KINGDOM WEALTH

UNDERSTANDING, ACCESSING AND EXPERIENCING THE LIFE GOD ORIGINALLY PURPOSED FOR YOU!

Kingdom Blessings

Prophetess Nicole [illegible]

Kingdom Wealth

NICOLE K. ARMSTRONG

ARMSTRONG GLOBAL PUBLISHING
P.O. BOX 742794
RIVERDALE, GA 30296

Kingdom Wealth by Nicole K. Armstrong
Published by Armstrong Global Publishing
P.O. Box 747294
Riverdale, Georgia 30296
Email: info@nicolearmstrong.org

Unless otherwise noted, all Scriptures quotations are from the KING JAMES VERSION of the Bible.

ISBN: 978-0-615-50453-7

Cover Design by Armando Hill
Email: higherglyph@gmail.com

Front Cover Photo by Reggie Anderson

Dedication

This book is dedicated to my grandmother, Rosline Victoria McLish, for her faith in God and for being one of the greatest intercessors and prayer warriors I will ever know; my wonderful mother Thelma Miller for her love and support. To my dearest son Nicholas Shepherd: you were born to be a great man of purpose and to be a leader. To my little sister Melissa Branch, one of my greatest encouragers and best friend. Thank you for always supporting me. To my brother, Andre Branch, a man of wisdom and knowledge. Also, to my aunt, Norma Castell, who also encourages me to continue the work God has for me.

FOREWORD

With the world's current economic climate, I am thoroughly convinced that Nicole Armstrong's release of *Kingdom Wealth* embodies a "sure" word for the times. She is more than qualified to expound on Kingdom wealth because of her many years of operating in the prophetic, serenading the Lord in worship, absorbing His word and lying on her face in prayer. Nicole has her fingers on the pulse of the Kingdom of God and is spiritually attuned to what the Body of Christ and our world needs in these End Times. I can say these things about Nicole, firsthand, because I have watched her "go forth" under the anointing and in a variety of ministry settings.

Throughout my many years of service as a Senior Pastor, I have heard the term Kingdom wealth countless times. It has a certain ring to it that makes one feel privileged to be a citizen of God's Kingdom. Although a vast number of people are familiar with the term, there are still those who do not have a clear understanding of it. Well, in this presentation, Nicole offers an in-depth treatment of this multifaceted phenomenon.

Nicole Armstrong's *Kingdom Wealth* hits the spiritual bull's-eye with such profound and thought-provoking principles as: "Kingdom wealth is about prospering in every area of your life...it's about becoming Kingdom investors...it's about living a life of integrity...it's about empowering others." I am confident that the rich nuggets found in this book will be preached from pulpits, taught in biblical study groups, meditated upon and committed to memory continuously by untold masses of people.

I salute my spiritual daughter, Prophetess Nicole Armstrong, for penning such an outstanding book and eagerly await her next project. May wealth and riches continue to reside in her house.

Bishop D. R. Collins, M.Div.
Faith Walk Ministries, Inc.
College Park, Georgia

Acknowledgements

First and foremost, I would like to thank my Lord and Savior Jesus Christ for saving me and filling me with His wonderful Holy Spirit. I thank God for choosing me to be His "prophetic voice preaching a kingdom message." This book was birthed in my spirit early one morning after my prayer time with the Lord. He deposited a message into my spirit immediately as I came out of prayer, and I began to write as the Holy Spirit spoke.

I do not have enough words to express my gratitude and appreciation to all the individuals who have helped me bring this book into manifestation, such as my cover designer, photographer, editor, advisor and big sister Evangelist Tracy Hunt; and also, to my dear friend and armorbearer Lisa Drayton, for your words of encouragement and prayers. To one of the greatest women of God I know, my mother Thelma Miller, thank you. For while I was yet in your womb you prayed for me and gave me back to God. MOM, thank you for being my warrior and intercessor.

I am especially grateful to God for giving me one of the greatest spiritual mothers, Bishop Dianne Collins. You are one of the most outstanding women of God I know. I have learned and gleaned so much from you. I thank you for seeing the call of God on my life, and for allowing God to use you in so many different ways to help push me into my destiny. There are no words to say to YOU how much I appreciate and love you.

A special thank you to Kay Thompson of Messenger Media Group. Special thanks to all my fellow ministerial colleagues and friends in the Gospel for their prayers, encouragement and acts of kindness.

Contents

Introduction

God has a plan for all of us. It does not matter where you have been and what you have done, it is about where you are now that determines where you are going. I understand that no two individuals stand at the same place in life and destiny. We all find ourselves at different places in our journey, but that does not mean that any of us are exempt from God's ordained plan for our lives. One of the greatest blessings that we all have and possess is the gift of life; and where there is life there is hope. It is never too late to change from who you have become to who God originally created you to be.

In this book, *Kingdom Wealth*, I will help you to understand, access and experience the life God originally ordained for you. The Bible says, **"Wisdom is the principle thing; therefore get wisdom: and with all thy getting get understanding" (Proverbs 4:7).** Kingdom wealth is about gaining the wisdom and understanding of who we are in God and what God has for us. If we can gain the understanding of God's plan for all of us, then it will become an essential tool for maximizing our purpose in Him. In addition, if we access it then certainly we will enjoy it.

I am aware of the various differences in the lives of the readers of this book. I know there are many of you who have been in ministry for years, and others that have never been in ministry. Some of you have already ministered around the world and some have never been outside of your local church. Also, there will be some of you that have never been outside of your country, state, city, region or territory in which you were born, but that does not mean that the wealth of the Kingdom is not available for you to access. No one, regardless of your status or position, has reached their limit in receiving from the abundance of God nor has reached a place in their life and journey where there is no more room for God to do something new in their soul, spirit and body. It does not matter how much or how little you have accomplished—how much or how little you have done—there is still more that God has for you.

Kingdom Wealth is a book that speaks to the very core of your being. This is a book that will bring you into a place of total wealth in your soul, spirit and body. We are not considered wealthy, according to God's standards, if our souls and character are not in alignment with His word. We all have been given a Kingdom assignment that is attached to a Kingdom schedule that must come into full manifestation according to God's Kingdom timing. Through Jesus Christ, we have been born again into the greatest Kingdom you can ever imagine. In God's Kingdom, we are all called to a destiny of greatness. Kingdom wealth is all about being the nation of people we were originally ordained to be. It is yours if you want it. Now, let's take this journey together!

A Global Message for a Kingdom People!

Prophetess Nicole K. Armstrong

Chapter I

Knowing Your Kingdom Position

Every person born into the earth realm has an attached purpose. You are not here by accident, no matter how conception took place. My purpose might not be your purpose, but it does not mean you do not have purpose. God went a step further, beyond purpose, and attached His Kingdom assignments to our purpose, giving us destiny. Jesus Christ came to earth to establish the Kingdom of God and to reestablish God's original plan for everyone. As a believer in Jesus Christ, we have a right to the wealth, riches and resources that God has given us to enjoy. However, outside of Christ, your true purpose can never be fully realized. Now, it is normal for us to think that our accomplishments define our purpose; however, true purpose does not manifest outside of Christ.

Many perceive their natural accomplishments in life as being their God-given purpose, and perhaps this may be true to a certain point; however, with some, God has assigned a purpose that may be coupled with natural accomplishments. People living outside of God's Kingdom might think they are fulfilling their God-ordained purpose. But I want to submit to you that true purpose can only be accomplished in God through Jesus Christ, by the enabling power of the Holy Spirit. Attaining earthly riches and fame does not mean you have obtained your spiritual inheritance, or that you have accomplished your purpose. You begin to accomplish God-ordained purpose in life when everything that you do is about God.

The Holy Spirit is our ultimate guide to helping us accomplish our destiny; giving Him full control will allow us to give God all the glory in all things.

When God created Adam and Eve, He gave them everything they needed to live in abundance; but because of disobedience, many things changed and shifted. Now notice I said "changed and shifted." We went from total relationship with God to a broken relationship with God (sin entered the world). We went from abundance to lack—first in our spirits, then in our souls and bodies, and finally in the earth. This is the progressive stage of the spirit of lack and poverty. Sickness and disease eventually began to manifest because of sin. Once man became disconnected from God spiritually, the soul became entangled with sinful thoughts, desires, self-will and emotions. Once the soul became corrupted, our physical bodies began to feel the effects of sin. Our body will always respond to what happens in our soul, and our soul will respond to our spirit.

Sin caused man to become deprived and disconnected. Sin caused lack and poverty to enter into the earth realm. Sin is the cause of sickness and disease. The effects of sin have caused such a devastating effect on the earth realm to the degree that the earth is still mourning for the manifestation of the sons of God. So, we see that poverty is not of God, lack is not of God and being poor is certainly not of God. The enemy deceived Adam and Eve because he needed a way to hold God's beautiful creation in bondage and poverty, and he wanted us to serve him instead of God. Because he lost all his privileges, he wanted us to do the same. Satan understood that in order to achieve this, he would have to deceive Adam and Eve into disobeying God—disconnecting all humanity from God. This is still the case now.

Every disconnected spirit is a deprived soul. The enemy always operates with the spirit of deception and distraction in an attempt to cause us to sin and disobey God. Sin is the entryway into our soul for the enemy to destroy us and keep us from obtaining our blessings from God. The enemy's sole purpose is to continuously keep us disconnected from God by any means. Sin caused us to be disconnected from God; this was not God's original plan for us. God is so wise, loving and faithful that when the enemy deceived Adam and Eve into sin, he thought that it was over for us with God. But God already had the plan of salvation in His mind.

We were created by God to know God and to be in eternal relationship with Him. We were also created to have a life of abundance, peace, joy and blessings. We were created for God's purpose: to continuously discover His greatness and splendor, the beauty of His majesty and the glory of His presence. We were created to praise and worship Him. The devil was jealous and full of pride—he wanted what God had. **"Now thanks be unto God, which always causeth us to triumph in Christ" (2 Corinthians 2:14a).**

Sin entered the world and man became a deprived soul and a disconnected spirit. But through Jesus Christ, salvation brought us back in connection with God and began the process of restoration. Christ came to reconnect that which was disconnected. Salvation is more than just praying the prayer of repentance. There is a supernatural act between God and us that has happened and will happen in the lives of everyone who accepts Jesus Christ as Savior and Lord. In the process of praying to God for forgiveness of your sins and accepting Jesus Christ as your Savior, the Holy Spirit immediately begins to cause your spirit to be regenerated and reconnected back to God.

God is always at work—He did not leave us without an answer. However, it is necessary for me to help you understand why there is a need for us to be restored back to God's original plan for our lives. In the Garden of Eden, after Adam and Eve sinned, God punished them both. They received consequences for their act of disobedience, but they did not lose their blessings: **"And God blessed them" (Genesis 1:28a).** Nowhere in scripture will you find that God removed His blessings from them. Neither has God removed the blessings He bestowed upon us.

God never took away their ability to walk in purpose, instead He said, **"In sorrow shalt thou eat of it all the days of thy life" (Genesis 3:17d)** and **"In sweat of thy face shalt thou eat bread" (Genesis 3:19a).** This means that which was at first freely given to you must now be worked for. This does not mean that you will not have provision. I tell you again, you just have to work for it. God's original intention for us was not to work so hard, or be in lack, need or poverty of any kind. Because of sin, we began to lack naturally, spiritually and emotionally.

Poverty is about more than just not having money; it is a form of lack and bondage in any area of your life. Poverty is working hard and never achieving anything; poverty is having enough and never sharing with someone in need. Lastly, spiritual poverty is settling for little when you can have much. Yes, at this point I know many of you will say, "But if Christ came to restore unto us our relationship with God then why are we still in this place of lack?"

The question is, once we become born again, why are there so many Christians who still lack emotionally, spiritually and physically? Well, the answer is threefold: first, lack of knowledge; next, lack of obedience; and third, having a wrong mindset, or never really coming into the full knowledge of who we are and whose we are. Jesus came to restore us back to our rightful place in the Kingdom of God. Our Kingdom place is one of abundance, wealth, dominion, fruitfulness, multiplication, replenishing and subduing. Jesus took us from a place of darkness into His light. We have been taken from a place of poverty to being positioned in His Kingdom wealth—the place of all sufficiency in Him.

> **And God blessed them, and God said unto them, Be fruitful, and multiply, and replenish the earth, and subdue it: and have dominion over the fish of the sea, and the over the fowl of the air, and over every living thing that moveth upon the earth. (Genesis 1:28)**

Let's define the blessings of God for us. I call them the **Five Principles of Success:**

- **I.** **Fruitful**—To produce; producing and abudant growth; productive of good result
- **II.** **Multiply**—To increase in number; quantity or extent; to perform the process of multiplication.
- **III.** **Replenish**—To make full or complete again; to supply again or afresh
- **IV.** **Subdue**—To conquer and bring into subjection; to control or claim; to defeat, subjugate, vanquish
- **V.** **Dominion**—Rule, supreme or sovereign authority; realm or domain

Notice there are five things God said for us to do, and many people I know that have followed these five principles have achieved some level of financial success.

***Note:** Principles work for the saved as well as the unsaved. However, by using the **Five Principles of Success** in your life, you can become rich. But one must have the Spirit of Christ to become wealthy.

Being fruitful is a state of flourishing. When we flourish we grow in a vigorous state—we increase by natural development. When we flourish we will also gain influence in every area of our life. We have everything we need to flourish and produce good results. It is our God-given right to be productive and flourishing.

As we flourish, we must multiply who we are and what we do. Every successful person understands that there must be an increase in their life to sustain their state of wealth. Once we understand the law of increase, we must also know how to activate the blessing of replenishing, allowing that which we have to always make full and provide a continuous flow and supply.

We are called to subdue. In other words, we have the ability to conquer everything that is a hindrance to us; and we must take control of every negative thought, word and action that will hinder us. God has given us a gift to dominate, meaning we should be the best at what we do and strive to be excellent at that which God has called us to do—without fear and doubt. God wants us to be the greatest, this is why He has blessed us to be fruitful, multiply, replenish, subdue and have dominion. (Genesis 1:28) There is room for every person to dominate the earth; we have all been given our regions and territories to be the best and the greatest in our Kingdom position.

We are called to be a Kingdom people with power to influence every aspect of society. The world is ours to control and establish His Kingdom if we use the wisdom of God to do it. Nothing is impossible to you once you understand who you have been called and blessed to be by God. God made us this way, so there is no need to apologize.

God went on to say that He has given unto us everything we need to be wealthy, healthy and live in abundance.

> **And God said, Behold, I have given you every herb bearing seed, which is upon**

> **the face of all the earth, and every tree, in the which is the fruit of a tree yielding seed; to you it shall be for meat. And to every beast of the earth, and to every fowl of the air, and to every thing that creepeth upon the earth, wherein there is life, I have given every green herb for meat: and it was so. And God saw every thing that he had made, and, behold, it was very good. And the evening and the morning were the sixth day. (Genesis 1:29-31)**

Success is not by chance or wishful thinking, it comes to everyone who works the Word and principles of God. In the book of Genesis, we see that from the creation of man, God already set in the earth the principles that will bring us wealth. It is good to think of yourself as wealthy, successful and great, because I do believe that true wealth begins with our thoughts and attitude. When we put our thoughts with our words and our words with our actions, the manifestation will occur. The wealth of the Kingdom of God is about who we are and what He has given to us. Kingdom wealth goes beyond your money; it is more about a person's being, not what they have.

Here are the defined words from the *Randon House Dictionary of the English Language* to help you come into a better understanding of Kingdom wealth.

Wealth is defined as abundance or profusion of anything plentiful; a great quantity of money or property of value; plentiful amount.

Wealthy is defined as rich in character, quality, or amount abundant or ample; a novel that wealthy is its psychological insight; prosperous, having great wealth, rich, affluent; a wealthy person, and a wealthy nation; characterized by pertaining to or suggestive of wealth; a wealthy appearance.

Kingdom is defined as the state, realm or domain ruled by a king or queen. A realm is the domain, including the subjects over which the king has jurisdiction; a sphere of power or influence; the domain over which the spiritual sovereignty of God or Christ extends, whether in heaven or in earth.

Kingdom Wealth is defined as a sphere and domain which the spiritual sovereignty of God rules, which entitles His subjects to have a sphere of power and influence; great abundance, rich in character, and affluent in society.

THE FORMULA FOR KINGDOM WEALTH

Right thinking + principled living (operating in the divine principles of God's word) + upholding God's standard of righteousness + wisdom, knowledge and understanding + tapping into purpose + preparation (actions) + obedience to God's word = Kingdom wealth.

Notice, if you have one without the other it will not produce Kingdom wealth. One might have money, but that does not mean that they are wealthy according to Kingdom standards. There is a wealth that is reserved for Kingdom citizens that is about more than having money. Remember, God is the one who gives us the power and ability to get wealth. **"But thou shalt remember the LORD thy God: for it is he that giveth thee power to get wealth [not money only], that he may establish his covenant which he sware unto thy fathers, as it is this day" (Deuteronomy 8:18).**

We have the ability to get wealth, but along with the ability must come action. In other words, we must do something. Not all Kingdom citizens are given the same giftings, but whatever God has given you has the power and potential to make you wealthy. Understanding who we are and what we have been given is necessary for us to experience the abundance of God. Having wealth and success was and still is a part of God's plan for our lives. We should never feel that God does not want us to be successful, because He does. God wants us to experience the abundance in every area of our life. Throughout the Bible, we see the promise of God linked with our obedience to Him. God did not reverse His blessings towards us, but to obtain the fullness of the blessing we must meet His requirements.

We must understand that we are kings and queens in the earth, with the power and ability to rule and have authority. However, it is necessary to know that all of this is accessible to us when we seek His righteousness and live according to His standards. As Kingdom citizens, we have access to the wealth of the Kingdom in the earth. Everything that we will ever need has already been provided by God. Never think that it is the will of God for you to live a life in lack; this is a trick of the enemy. God is a God of abundance and blessings. We are His Kingdom citizens, and as citizens of the Kingdom, we can access everything that belongs to us.

WE ARE CREATED FOR GREATNESS!
ALL THAT WE NEED IS ALREADY
PROVIDED!

Chapter II

Understanding Your Kingdom Benefits

All Kingdom citizens have rights, benefits and privileges given to us by Christ our King; however, many of us live as if we do not have any at all. Why? Because of a lack of knowledge: **"My people are destroyed for the lack of knowledge" (Hosea 4:6a).** Think about a person who has worked on the same job for years. They have great health benefits but never use them. When they get sick and go to the doctor, they pay for their care out-of-pocket. They spend thousands of dollars but never use the coverage available to them because of the lack of understanding about their employee benefits. This sounds unheard of in today's time, doesn't it? However, I want to submit to you that because of lack of knowledge, so many believers are paying daily because they are not using the benefits given to them by God as Kingdom citizens.

The moment a person receives salvation from Jesus Christ, he or she automatically becomes a citizen of the Kingdom of God. And, as citizens, we have rights, privileges and benefits. In order to have full access and rights to our benefits and privileges, we must come to a better understanding of who we are and what we have been given. It is the will of God for us to not only know our rights, but also to experience the benefits from them.

There are several steps to help us maximize on the blessings of being in the Kingdom of God. The first step to receiving your God-given privileges is knowing your rights!

All nations and kingdoms contain inherent principles and laws that must be adhered to by each citizen in order for them to receive the benefits of their citizenship. In the Kingdom, these rights are called keys of the Kingdom. As Kingdom citizens, we need keys "of" the Kingdom, not "to" the Kingdom—we are already "in" the Kingdom. Kingdom citizens already have keys to access the wealth that God has given, simply by being a Kingdom citizen.

There are several keys we have, but just having them is not sufficient for us to receive the benefits of them. If we do not use our keys, we will never gain access to the abundance of wealth that is intended for us. Remember, keys give access and we have access to the things of God through our Kingdom keys or rights. The keys of the Kingdom unlock the power of the Kingdom and cause our lives to align with our rightful inheritance in God.

God has given us the scriptures and the Holy Spirit, which together help the believer know how to access and live in their rights. To have the keys of the Kingdom is to have the knowledge of the Kingdom and access to the things of God. Keys represent several things, such as access, authority, ownership, power and, most of all, freedom to enter and exit a place at will. Just having the keys and not using them will not benefit us. We must use the keys of the Kingdom of Heaven to have access and experience the wealth of God in our lives.

Keys are principles found in the scriptures. They teach us how the Kingdom of God operates; and without these keys, we will not access the Kingdom of God. In the natural, if your house or car is locked, without keys you cannot access either of them. It is the same in the Kingdom of God. We cannot access the Kingdom without using the keys given to us in scripture.

Here are several Kingdom keys that we have: a) Faith, b) Scriptures, c) Prayer, d) Praise, e) Worship, f) Fasting, g) Holiness, h) Wisdom, i) Obedience, and j) Knowledge of the Word of God. These are just some of the keys of the Kingdom of God. This is not intended to be an exhaustive list but a reference for further study of the scriptures.

The second step is to understand your benefits! **"Blessed be the Lord, who daily loadeth us with benefits, even the God of our salvation" (Psalm 68:19).** As Kingdom citizens, we are supposed to operate at a level that will blow the mind of the world and not the believer. The world is supposed to stop and take notice of the believers. But believers are taking notice of the world, because many of us do not understand our benefits. We are living beneath our means and thus envying the world when we are suppose to provoke the world to godly jealously.

When we operate in God's power and authority, we allow the Holy Spirit to govern our actions. When this happens, we will have mind-blowing blessings. There is nothing we cannot accomplish as Kingdom citizens! We need to take the limits off of God and ourselves. It does not matter at this point where you find yourself in life; we are all called to live at a level of Kingdom wealth that will have the world wanting to know more about us as a Kingdom people. The world will ask us how we did that, instead of us asking the world.

Living the life God originally intended for us is one of the believers' greatest tools for witnessing to the unsaved. Kingdom wealth is not just designed for you to have all the abundance of God and that's it, but it is also designed to be a tool that the Holy Spirit can use in the earth to win souls to the Kingdom. Kingdom wealth is not just about the money, but it is about the lifestyle of godliness, peace and joy in the Holy Ghost. Apart from living in your Kingdom wealth is the peace of mind that comes from God—this cannot be attained outside of your relationship with Him. Every single individual that is living desires such peace and joy; and when we show the world the real peace that comes from God, we show them a life that is to be desired. We are the "salt of the earth, the light of the world," and that allows us to shine and flavor the world with God's glory.

Another benefit is that we will have no lack in our lives! **Psalm 23:1 says: "The Lord is my shepherd I shall not want."** If we lack, this is because we are not allowing the Shepherd to guide us. We are not supposed to have any lack in our money, relationships, health or substance. The word of God clearly states this. It is time to give God control of those areas where there is lack and let His abundance come in. To access the abundance of God in our lives we must trust His leading, instructions and directions. God owns everything—He has everything we will ever need in this life and the one to come.

The Bible states: **"The earth is the Lord's and the fullness thereof, the world and they that dwell therein" (Psalm 24:1).** He knows where to lead us to receive our abundant supply. No, God is not in the business of withholding things from us. It is God's pleasure to supply all our needs according to His riches in glory. Remember, God never intended for us to lack. **"For the Lord God is a sun and shield: the Lord will give grace and glory: no good thing will he withhold from them that walk uprightly" (Psalm 84:11).**

The Bible states: **"Trust in the Lord with all thine heart; and lean not unto thine own understanding. In all thy ways**

acknowledge him, and he shall direct thy paths" (Proverbs 3:5-6). We are supposed to be living life at a level where we are tapping into resources that cannot be explained: this is called **"Unexplainable Favor."** Having unexplainable favor allows us to live life on another dimension—above the world's standard of wealth and success. To receive the benefits of being in the Kingdom, you must know how to use your keys in the locks God provides for your prosperity, health, peace, joy, relationships, authority and money (yes money!).

Having the right key will open the warehouse of Heaven and cause your blessings to overtake you until you have no room to receive them. Following the instructions of God is not a request but a requirement to obtaining all that He has for you. The Bible says anything you ask in the name of Jesus will and shall be done—according to His will and purpose. **"Ask, and it shall be given you; seek, and ye shall find; knock, and it shall be opened unto you: For every one that asketh receiveth; and he that seeketh findeth; and to him that knocketh it shall be opened" (Matthew 7:7-8).**

We are so glad that it is His will for us to be prosperous in every area of our life. God clearly states that He desires for us to live a life filled with His blessings. Remember, **"the earth is the Lord's and the fullness thereof" (Psalm 24:1a).** The plans and thoughts of the Lord are good and of peace. God thinks about us: **"For I know the thoughts that I think toward you, saith the Lord, thoughts of peace, and not of evil, to give you an expected end" (Jeremiah 29:11).**

How awesome it is to know that God thinks about us with thoughts of peace and not evil, to give us an expected end. We can expect the goodness of God to overtake us; we can expect the blessings of God to shower down on us; we can expect the favor of God to surround us; and we can expect the peace of God to flood our hearts and minds. We can expect God to be faithful towards us. We can expect the word of God to be fulfilled in our lives. Raise your expectations of God and expect Him to do for you that which He promises. Every day you live, expect God to do something good for you. Every morning you rise, expect God to bless you.

God is faithful to His word: **"God is not a man, that he should lie; neither the son of man, that he should repent: hath he said, and shall he not do it? or hath he spoken, and shall he not make it good?" (Numbers 23:19).** Expect God to be God in your life. **"My soul, wait thou only upon God; for my expectation is from him" (Psalm 62:5).**

Use Your Privileges!

A privilege is a special right or benefit enjoyed by a particular person or group. As Kingdom citizens, we are that particular group called, according to the Word, "peculiar people." (1 Peter 2:9) So, to walk in our privileges, we must first let go of the mindset of poverty and lack. Know that it is our right to be wealthy and healthy. When Adam and Eve sinned, God did not tell them they would no longer have a right to the earth, He just told them that there would now be some consequences they must endure. God then immediately implemented a plan of restoration. (Genesis 3:15)

We see that God did not take away our privileges; we do have divine privileges from God. When God was about to give the children of Israel the Promised Land, He reminded Joshua of His promise toward him and His people. Even though God gave Joshua and the children of Israel the land, they still had to fight the enemies that were living in that land. Even though God wants us to be prosperous, we still have to work, fight the enemy of our faith, speak the word of God, and have total faith, trust and confidence in God. We are destined to win if we rely on God and God alone. We have a right and authority to everything that God gave to us: never let anything or anyone stop you from going after your rightful inheritance.

We have so many promises from God in the scriptures, but we still have to fight for them. We must fight fear (one of our biggest enemies), doubt, insecurity, low self-esteem, pride, depression, oppression, greed, etc. Victory belongs to us! We are not fighting for the victory; we are fighting to maintain the victory we already have been given through Jesus Christ. When any situation arises that might make you feel defeated, know that you have already won and all you have to do is declare your victory.

We have been given the power to overcome through the shed blood of Jesus and the indwelling presence of the Holy Spirit. We cannot enjoy the abundance of God if we do not fight the enemy's tricks, plans and tactics against our soul (will, mind, emotions, desires, intellect); our greatest warfare is in our mind. We must understand that if the enemy can distort our mind or thinking, he can interfere with our Kingdom wealth (the life of abundance from God).

God's instructions and commands remain the same to us today: we are to fight the enemy by being strong and of good courage. Never be afraid or dismayed. **"Have not I commanded thee [us]? Be strong and of a good courage; be not afraid, neither be thou dismayed: for the Lord thy God is with thee whithersoever thou goest" (Joshua 1:9).** This command is not limited to a country, region or territory. Wherever you live you have access to the rights, benefits and privileges given to you by God. But wherever you are, you must be strong and of good courage—you cannot be afraid or dismayed, because God is with you. Your success and wealth is not confined to just a country—your Kingdom wealth can be accessed on any area of the globe. God has given us regions and territories, and in these places shall all nations call you blessed. God's abundance is available to all believers globally; the power of God can destroy any spirit of lack, poverty, sickness or disease, wherever it exists.

The Bible lets us know it is the anointing that destroys the yoke: **"And it shall come to pass in that day, that his burden shall be taken away from off thy shoulder, and his yoke from off thy neck, and the yoke shall be destroyed because of the anointing" (Isaiah 10:27).** If the anointing is released in your region, the yoke will be destroyed. There is a difference between the breaking of something and the destruction of it. When something is broken, it has the potential to return. When something is destroyed, it will not return. We want every spirit of the enemy that has been assigned to hinder you, your country or region from experiencing Kingdom wealth, in every area, to be destroyed.

God's wealth is for His Kingdom citizens globally. It doesn't matter how poor your country might be, you can still live a life of abundance because the anointing of wealth and prosperity will destroy the yoke of poverty, if you use it. Remember, it is the anointing that destroys every yoke! So if you find yourself in a region that you might feel is not conducive to you obtaining your Kingdom wealth, begin to attack the spirit of the enemy that is holding back the prosperity of that region, in Jesus' name.

REMEMBER, THE SPIRIT OF POVERTY IS NOT FROM GOD!

Pray This Prayer

Father I ask you, in the name of Jesus, to release the anointing in this region that will destroy the yoke of lack and poverty. I apply the blood of Jesus over my home, family, finances and every resource that belongs to me. I command that the spirit of poverty go now in the name of Jesus. I now receive the prosperity of God in my life. I thank you Father and praise you for destroying every yoke in every area of my life, today and forevermore.

"In the house of the righteous is much treasure: but in the revenues of the wicked is trouble" (Proverbs 15:6). "A good man leaveth an inheritance to his children's children: and the wealth of the sinner is laid up for the just" (Proverbs 13:22).

KINGDOM PRINCIPLES FOR LIVING! GOD'S ORIGINAL DESIGN FOR US WAS TO BE FRUITFUL, NOT FRUITLESS!

Chapter III

Unlocking the Door to Kingdom Finances!!!

Knowledge without application is fruitless, and God wants us to be fruitful. It is now my challenge to speak to the Kingdom citizens to use the principles given to us by God to move from barrenness to productivity, from lack to abundance, from emptiness to overflow. The word unlock is defined as to open or unfasten by releasing, to reveal or disclose. Unlocking is an action word, which means using what God gave us to open and release that which is tied up.

Actions coupled with the principles of God's word work when we work them. Tithing, giving and sowing are three of the keys to releasing that which has been held up. In order to understand how to access the wealth of the Kingdom, there are several Kingdom requirements necessary for discussion. The first area of wealth I will discuss is how to obtain the abundance in our finances.

Now let us look at what the Word says—it is time to work the Word! Using the principles found within the scriptures will bring us into our place of financial wealth. Understand that Kingdom wealth is more than money; however, having money is a part of it. The Bible says: **"Bring ye all the tithes into the storehouse, that there may be meat in mine house, and prove me now herewith, saith the Lord of hosts, If I will not open you the windows of heaven,**

and pour you out a blessing, that there shall not be room enough to receive it" (Malachi 3:10).

Tithes

Tithes are necessary for protection for every Kingdom citizen. Tithing is the practice of giving 10% of your income to the Lord; this is called storehouse tithing. Tithes are your taxes that you pay to God to live in His earth and enjoy His rights, benefits and privileges. Tithing is not optional, it is a requirement.

IN KINGDOM TITHING, WE ALSO TITHE OUR TIME AND GIFTINGS, ALONG WITH OUR MONEY!

Giving God our time is very important as well. God has given us twenty-four hours in a day, and out of that day we should make sure we give God at least two hours and forty minutes. Then we should give God another two hours as an offering of our time. Many of us reading this are saying, "WOW, that is a lot of time." But can I submit to you that we should give God more time than anything or anyone. We can never spend too much time with the Lord. The more of ourselves we give God, the more of Him we will have—the more we will become like Him, the more we will sound like Him and the more we will do for Him. Oh, I thank you Jesus!

Examples of the Benefits of Tithing

Whenever we work any form of a job, we are required to pay taxes. Taxes are not a request but are a requirement from the government. There is a system already in place that is able to accommodate all taxpayers. It is the law that every person receiving an income must pay their taxes. Even though you are required to pay taxes, there are still benefits that are received from paying them.

Before you get your check from your employer, taxes have already been taken out. If you are self-employed, you are required to pay taxes on your earnings, otherwise you will suffer the consequence of not paying taxes to the government. If your house was on fire and you called the fire department, they would come as quickly as possible to extinguish it. After the fire has been put out, the fire department does not turn around and bill you for coming. WHY? Because your taxes have taken care of their pay. The same is true with the police department. They are paid from our taxes to protect us. Taxes are necessary to keep our society flowing right.

I liken tithes to Kingdom taxes. Just as it is necessary to pay taxes, it is doubly necessary that all Kingdom citizens pay their tithes. God has already given us instructions on how to pay our tithes. He already has a system in place to accommodate us. As it is in the natural, so also in the spiritual—tithing is a natural act that produces spiritual benefits. Tithing provides so many benefits, blessings and advantages. Not paying your tithes will cause great disadvantages.

Tithing is a significant key to opening and unlocking the Kingdom's warehouse of blessings. Blessing are not something that you can buy—they are what God gives. God's protection is a blessing, God's provision is a blessing and God's favor is a blessing. The ability to prosper is also a blessing. All these blessings cannot be earned or bought; they can only be obtained through obedience. The paying of your tithes provides so many blessings from God to Kingdom citizens.

Situations in our lives will always occur, but when they do, you should know that you have protection from God if you are a consistent tithe payer. There is a blessing in being obedient to God in every area of our lives. Kingdom wealth is about living the life God originally ordained for us—total obedience is the only way to live such a life. Why do we expect God to bless us if we are not obedient? We bring many things upon ourselves because of our disobedience. Deuteronomy 28 gives us a clear example of the blessings of obedience and the consequences (curses) of disobedience. Not paying your tithes is considered disobedience, according to **Malachi 3:9a: "Ye are cursed with a curse."** This is a serious consequence. To be cursed with a curse is a double curse! We always talk about the double portion blessings but never the double portion curse. When we do not bring the tithes into the house of the Lord, the Bible says that we **"are cursed with a curse: for ye have robbed me, even this whole nation" (Malachi 3:9).** Here are some curses that will happen because of not paying your tithes.

I. The devourer will not be rebuked. This means all of your money and possessions will be eaten up; there will be difficulty in saving; and, if you do try to save, situations will always occur that will take away your money or possessions. Your pockets will seem as if they have holes in them—every time you get money it will seem to disappear just as quickly as it appeared. This will make you frustrated because it will appear as if you never have enough to do what you need to do, i.e., pay bills, buy food.

II. The devourer will destroy the fruit of your ground, business, job, investments, bank account, ministry, etc. It all will be affected. All of your money will be eaten up over and over again. Every time you get increase, it will decrease just as fast as it comes.

III. Things will not last, and the ground will cast out the fruit before its time. Things you try to work for will be destroyed. The level of success desired will not be attained—things will prematurely fall apart. Your business will struggle and your bank account will appear as if you cannot maintain a significant balance.

But we thank God that the obedience of paying our tithes is better than not paying. As long as we are tithe payers, we will never have to worry about being cursed. **"And I will rebuke the devourer for your sakes, and he shall not destroy the fruits of your ground; neither shall your vine cast her fruit before the time in the field, saith the Lord of hosts" (Malachi 3:11).** Here are the blessings associated with paying your tithes.

I. The devourer will be rebuked (your money will multiply and situations will not always take away your money or possessions). You will always have what you need.

II. The devourer will not destroy the fruit of your ground (ministry, business, job, investments, bank accounts, etc., will not be affected). Your business will reach a place of flourishing and multiplication.

III. The fruit of your ground will last and produce a proper harvest. Your bank account will see an increase and things that you try to do (business, investments, jobs, ministry) will work in your favor.

God has given us protection and provision through the obedient act of paying tithes. Tithes are Kingdom taxes; and it is not a request from God to pay your tithes, it is a requirement. Tithing causes that which is left over, your 90%, to be blessed and go the distance. When you pay your tithes you release the blessings of the Lord upon your life, business, job, ministry, bank accounts, investments and everything that is connected to you.

Tithes should be paid where you worship, such as your local church. If you do not have a local church, I would recommend that you find one so you can obtain the blessings that come from not only being a faithful giver, but also from being connected to fellow believers. It is not good to be without a church home. Through times of fellowship, you will be able to continue to receive all the blessings that come from God.

There are so many benefits for you when you are connected to a body of believers, and these are often overlooked due to lack of understanding. You cannot get the same thing at home looking at television. There is a ministry out there for you; there is a pastor that God has assigned to you. We are not called to do our Kingdom assignment alone. I will discuss this further in my next book, *Kingdom Worshippers.* Now that we understand how to unlock the windows, let us look at how to get great abundance to pour out of the open windows.

The Offering

Offerings are what I call your Kingdom investments. This is where you will get a return on your seed. When you pay your tithes and give an offering, you have just put money into the account of Heaven that will bring you back a bountiful harvest. Tithing protects you and your seed or offering, so that the seed can grow and yield a return on it. The measure in which you give will be given back to you. Tithing opens up Heaven's window, but an offering will determine what comes out of the window. Many of us have gotten the window to open but have nothing coming out of the window because we limit our giving.

Please Note: you can never give too much but you can give too little. According to how the Lord has prospered you, that is how you ought to give. If you can give hundreds, thousands or millions give it, because it will always come back in a greater dimension than you gave. You give out of what you have, and always give your best; your increase comes through the release of your seed. In the next section on giving, I will discuss several other ways of giving that will cause floods of blessings and increase to come out of Heaven's window.

IF YOU WANT MONEY GIVE MONEY, AND YOU WILL GET BACK MONEY!

(But note that in Kingdom giving, we give more than money.)

If you want love give love, and you will receive love.
Give compassion and you will get compassion.
Become a true friend and give friendship, and you will get a true friend from the relationship.

If you give you will receive. Your gift will return to you in full measure, pressed down, shaken together and running over. Expect more and more. Whatever measure you use in giving—large or small—it will be used to measure what is given back to you. (Luke 6:38)

Giving is always tied to God's financial blessings. The above scripture is the principle to unlocking the door or window of Heaven. You must first adhere to this principle in order to see great manifestations in your life. In order to receive much we have to always go beyond the norm. The more the Lord gives you the more He requires of you. God will never require of you something you are unable to do and give.

There is nothing in the Bible that God requires of us that we are unable to do. Not doing something does not mean we cannot do it. Now, just because some of you are unable to give thousands at this time does not mean you will not be able to soon. But all of us can improve our giving, and I will show you how in the next section. But we are never to go before the Lord empty; always give some thing to the Lord and always make sure it is your best. **Deuteronomy 16:16c states: "They shall not appear before the Lord empty."**

God wants to bless us with everything we need, but we must follow the order of God. You see, there are laws that have been put in place, principles that must be followed for the blessing to overtake us. Appearing before the Lord empty is something God commanded us not to do. Every time we come before Him, come with our praise, worship and gift. Everything we need has already been provided; however, we must position ourselves to cause a release so that we can obtain.

Pray This Prayer

Father, in the name of Jesus, I come to you first to ask you to forgive me for my lack of stewardship over what you have given me. God, I want to repent for every time I withheld my tithes and offerings from you. God, I want to repent for every time I came before you and did not give you my best. God, I know that my best might not be the same as someone else's, and I will not compare myself to them; but God, I will from now on do my best. You have so many blessings for me, and I ask you to lead me and guide me so I can become the giver that you have blessed me to be. Thank you for being the All Sufficient One. God, I just want to take this time to give you the praise and worship you deserve. Amen.

APPLICATION IS ONE OF THE KEYS TO OBTAINING THE BLESSING!

Chapter IV

Kingdom Increase from the Principles of Giving!

SEED OFFERINGS

Seed offerings are a type of giving outside of your tithes and offerings. This type of giving is done when it is requested of you or when you want to be a blessing. These types of offerings are given at revivals, conferences, church services, ministry events or other venues. When God tells you to bless someone or you feel in your heart that you want to be blessing to an individual or individuals in a tangible way (money), this is also considered a seed offering.

I remember going to a conference and I sensed in my spirit that I should sow a seed in the life of the pastor hosting the conference. After I put the check in his hand, I began to feel a little intimidated because of the amount, and I started to apologize. Now it was a good amount of money for where I was financially at the time. It was not as big as what many others were sowing that day, and when he received my seed, I will never forget the words he said to me: "Never apologize for your seed!" I learned at that moment a lesson about giving that changed me. I could have missed the blessings that were assigned to that seed if I did not release it, simply because I thought it was not enough. But it was enough because it was my sacrifice. Now I am in a place that I can give a lot more than that, but that seed changed my thinking—that alone was a tremendous blessing.

"NEVER APOLOGIZE FOR YOUR SEED!"

Why should you never apologize for your seed? The answer is that no amount is too small or large: you control your seed, and the seed you give is voluntary. This type of seed giving is not based on the amount, but comes from your willingness to be a blessing in the life of someone else. Therefore, one should never apologize when volunteering to give a blessing. Remember, we give according to how the Lord has prospered us. If you are able to sow millions, thousands, hundreds or tens, then do so, but never limit or hinder yourself from sowing because you feel it is not enough.

We are Kingdom builders and when we sow our seeds into the life of another person or ministry, we should always see it as a Kingdom investment. No amount is too large or small. One million dollars is just like one dollar to those who have it. God can allow someone to give you millions just as easily as someone can give you hundreds, or ones. We put emphasis on the amount, not God. The sacrifice is what is honored, not necessarily the amount.

If you are a millionaire and only sow a hundred dollars, that is not much to you; however, someone who has a few hundred and sows one hundred dollars considers it a sacrifice. Understanding each person's level of sacrificial giving is different, so we should never be intimidated by what we sow based in comparison to what another person sows. We are always blessed to be a blessing, so our focus should always be geared toward how to be a blessing in any manner we can.

Seed Offering With an Assignment

A seed offering with an assignment is something that I realize many Christians are not aware of and, of course, do not practice. God instructed me some years ago to name the seeds that I sow into the Kingdom. This particular type of offering is given when you want God to move in a certain area of your life or situation: It is a **"Specific Request."**

For example, when a farmer sows corn at the time of harvest, he is not expecting broccoli because he knows what seed was sown. It is the same for us. If you sow apple seeds how can you expect oranges? After understanding this concept, the Holy Spirit began to say, "When you ask the people to sow a specific seed, instruct them to give the seed an assignment." We give our seeds assignments by naming them. Everything in the earth realm has an assignment—and we must attach purpose and assignment to our special seed.

If you want your house to be paid off, sow a seed on it; if you want your car to be paid off, sow a seed on it; if you want your business to flourish, sow a seed for it. This principle works. I have been doing this for some time and I have seen God do just what I sowed the seed for.

For those of you in ministry, begin to give your seeds assignments for what you believe God to do in your ministry. Attach a seed to your Kingdom assignment. If you believe God for a television ministry or for the expansion of your ministry, sow seeds for it. If you are believing God for open doors, sow your seed on it—but always name your seed offering.

Note: You cannot give your tithes assignments because they already have an assignment from God: 1) rebuke the devourer, and

2) open the windows of Heaven. As discussed above, there are many blessings that come from sowing your tithes. So this principle does not apply to your tithes, it applies to your offerings and seed offerings.

EVERY SEED SOWN NEEDS AN ASSIGNMENT!

God began to teach me about the principle of sowing a thousand dollar seed. It is easy for many to sow tens and even hundreds, but it is somewhat difficult for many of us to sow in the denomination of a thousand. There is something very significant about sowing the thousand dollar seed, because it puts you in a different harvest field. Not only that, but it also completely destroys the spirit of lack and poverty off your life. I call this the seed of breakthrough: the seed which completely shatters the enemy's hand off your finances. If you want God to move in your finances, quickly sow the seed of breakthrough.

The thousand dollar seed is the seed of breakthrough in your finances—permanently changing your financial status. The seed of breakthrough is the type of sowing that causes major doors to be opened and opportunities to come, because this seed instantly changes your status. If you are believing God to move you into MILLIONAIRE status, this is the seed that will do it. A thousand-fold return on a THOUSAND DOLLARS IS ONE MILLION DOLLARS. One seed can change your whole financial outlook; a thousand dollar seed will bring a thousand-fold return into your life.

Solomon was chosen to be the next king of Israel after his father David! He gave the Lord a sacrificial offering of a thousand burnt offerings and God responded to him.

> **And Solomon went up thither to the brasen altar before the Lord, which was at the tabernacle of the congregation, and offered a thousand burnt offerings upon it. In that night did God appear unto Solomon, and said unto him, Ask what I shall give thee. (2 Chronicles 1:6-7)**

Solomon's response was a great one, he asked God for wisdom to do his Kingdom assignment. He did not ask God for a selfish, self-centered blessing, but he put the needs of his people first. (2 Chronicles 1:10) God blessed Solomon with the wisdom he asked for, and God honored Solomon by giving him riches, wealth and honor like no one before or after him. (2 Chronicles 6:12) Let us look at the principles attached to Solomon's offering:

I) He had a Kingdom assignment because he was the next king of Israel.

II) His offering provoked a response from God that allowed him to receive from the Lord something no one ever had, nor will ever attain again.

We have a Kingdom assignment and our seeds of sacrifice and breakthrough will cause God to bless us with everything we need and more, just as he did with Solomon.

Once you are able to sow the seed of a thousand, then you should begin preparing yourself to sow the $10,000, $100,000 and $500,000 seed; and then the $1 million, $10 million and $20 million dollar seed, etc. We can always expect a thousand-fold return on our seeds of assignment. Many of you have already sown the seed of breakthrough and are experiencing great financial increase, but you are not exempt because each seed brings a different level of financial status. If you are already a millionaire, then sow in the denomination that will make you a billionaire in the Kingdom. Yes, I said "Billionaire."

We are given great financial wealth for the establishing and building of the Kingdom of God in the earth. We are called to establish His Kingdom in the earth. We have become and are becoming Kingdom "Millionaires and Billionaires" to fulfill our Kingdom assignments and focus on the Kingdom agenda. I believe that God is beginning to establish billionaires in the Kingdom because the assignments are greater for the next season of Kingdom work that is to be done.

We are called to influence the world, not become like the world. We cannot change the world for God if we accommodate it; we are called to be change agents. The church cannot become like the world system and culture, we are called to change. Jesus came to reintroduce His Kingdom to the world. Our Kingdom assignment is to continue the message of Jesus and finish His work. We are called out of the world to help change the world and establish the Kingdom of God—and we need finances to do it.

REMEMBER, IT'S TIME FOR THE WORLD TO NOTICE US INSTEAD OF US NOTICING THE WORLD!

LIVING A LIFE OF INTEGRITY IS NECESSARY TO EXPERIENCE KINGDOM WEALTH!

Chapter V

Kingdom Stockholders

KINGDOM INVESTMENTS

What are Kingdom investments? Before we answer this question, let's first define investment. An investment is defined as the investing of money for profitable returns; a property or right in which someone invests. Kingdom investors are those that invest their money into ministries that are doing Kingdom work for the return of souls. Souls are the greatest return on a Kingdom investment.

Kingdom wealth is about us obtaining everything we need from God to be effective Kingdom citizens. We are called to dominate and have influence in every aspect of society. Having God's status of wealth is necessary for this to be accomplished. As Kingdom citizens, we should set up our portfolio to invest into ministries that are reaching the world for Christ; these investors are also called ministry partners. We should not limit ourselves by how many ministries we invest in; when we partner with a ministry, we are investing into the ministry on behalf of Kingdom purpose.

Just like your earthly investment yields a return, your Kingdom investment will yield an eternal return, which is called your reward. Every time you help a ministry to evangelize the Gospel and souls are won, you get earned interest on your investment, which is recorded in Heaven. God has designed this life to extend into our eternal life. What we do on earth now for God will be rewarded when Christ returns as well. All the rewards we receive from our Kingdom investments are not only limited to when Christ returns, but there are rewards that we get now as well. We should not just look at our Kingdom investment for eternal rewards, we should expect some rewards in this life as well. God will not only provide for us while we live in the earth, but also when we go into eternity with Him. God's Kingdom is about now, as well as what is to come. We all can become Kingdom investors. There is no amount too great or too small for this investment. Kingdom investing is something we all can do and should want to do. No one should exempt themselves from the wonderful opportunities to make Kingdom investments.

Stockholders in the Kingdom (Kingdom Investors)

Invest means to put money to use in something or someone offering a profitable return; to use or devote time, talents, etc., as to achieve something; to cover, surround or to help establish. We become Kingdom investors when we invest into the lives of those individuals that have been called to the Kingdom and are doing Kingdom assignments.

We all have a Kingdom assignment, which has a Kingdom schedule, with a Kingdom agenda and is attached to Kingdom timing. God has a set time for all of us in which He will manifest His word in our lives, if we are obedient to His instructions. We should never be jealous of anyone when God blesses them because God has a time for everyone and He is not a "respecter of persons." We should always invest into the life of God's people; this is how we show our interdependence.

We are to invest into each other and not just ourselves; this is how we combine our gifting packages and make them work. I might not be able to do what you do, and you might not be able to do what I do, but together we make an impact and investment for Kingdom purposes. We can invest our time, talent, resources, and money in the life of someone else that is doing or wants to do Kingdom work.

KINGDOM INVESTORS DO NOT STAND ALONE!

Kingdom investors also use their influence and resources to help others in the Kingdom fulfill their Kingdom assignments. We cannot do it alone; God has not designed us to do His Kingdom work alone. WE NEED EACH OTHER. Many of us do not want to admit that we need the help or influence of others; but we do, and there is nothing wrong with admitting that we need the help of our fellow Kingdom citizens to do our assignment.

Now let's be clear: just because we make an investment, does not mean we are investors. Investors are not just onetime givers—they maintain a continuous cycle of giving and building. When we help someone to reach their place of destiny and walk in their purpose, we help them stand in their assignment. You do not stop, however, with that one individual, you allow God to send you another and another. Being a Kingdom investor is more than a onetime investment, but about multiple investments in the lives of Kingdom citizens.

We cannot become untouchable or unreachable if we are going to become Kingdom investors. The spirit of fame, stardom and celebrity must die. The Lone Ranger spirit must die, because we are not called to build the Kingdom and fulfill purpose alone.

The clicks and who's who circle must die. The spirit of intimidation and insecurity will be one of the biggest hindrances for many of us seeking to become Kingdom investors. We should never become intimidated, jealous or fearful of others' gifts. We should never deny ourselves the blessing of being a part of someone's life that God has called to be great in the Kingdom.

We are all Kingdom citizens and God has gifted us with the gifts He wants us to have. God gave each of us what He wanted us to have, so we are to be excited about our gifts and allow who we are to be a blessing to others. We are called to be great; no one is greater than the other. However, all of us are not called to do the same assignment, and our individual assignments will determine where we go and what we do. The doors that open and will be opened—the connections that have been made and will be made—are based on our Kingdom assignment.

We must not allow ourselves to operate in a spirit that says, "I made it, so now you need to do what it takes for you to make it." As the Bible says, there is no respecter of persons in God; we are all a part of the same Kingdom, serving the same King, going to the same place.

IT IS OUR KINGDOM DUTY TO INVEST IN OTHERS!

Bishops, apostles and senior pastors, it is time to invest in your inner circle of ministry leaders and other leaders that are not a part of your fellowship or church affiliation. When I say invest, I am referring to sowing seeds, time, talent and sharing influential resources. I know that many of you are praying for your leaders, training them and delegating various responsibilities to them. However, I believe this is the time to give back. Your investment will benefit the Kingdom of God; not just the local church. When your leaders receive a call to the Kingdom, they will need your prayers, encouragement, counsel and tangible support like never before.

God will send people into your church or ministry who are anointed, gifted and knowledgeable in the word of God and other areas of expertise for a season. Many times, leaders, you do not invest in these individuals because you are already aware of their brief tenure. But regardless of how long God will have them to serve under you, your assignment is to find ways to empower, equip and bless them, as well as utilize their giftings so that the Kingdom will benefit.

Most pastors desire to expand beyond the local church and have overlooked a proven way to do it—Kingdom investing. Apostles and senior pastors, the Kingdom of God is much bigger than your church, fellowship or organization. Jesus' message is a message of the Kingdom, not the church. However, the church was established to be an entity within the Kingdom. Investing of this type expands to all genre of leadership including business, civic, political or educational arenas. You are only as great as the people you have helped and will help to come into their Kingdom position.

If you are in a position of senior leadership and are already implementing this investment principle with the leaders inside and outside of your organization, I commend you. Someone took a leap of faith and invested in you, and look where you are today. Now it is your time to do the same for those God has placed under your care. Your obedience and giving spirit are a testament to the kind of leader you are. The Kingdom of God could use more people like you.

On the other hand, I am well aware that there are plenty of hirelings out there who are not worthy of such investments. They will drain you, your ministry or your organization financially, at every turn, if given the opportunity. This is where discernment and wisdom comes into play. It would be wise to not invest in such individuals because they have character issues that need to be addressed. Who knows, God may not want you to invest in their lives at this time because He desires to do a work in them first. This type of investment principle is not just limited to leaders, but to everyone that is a part of the Kingdom. We are to invest in each other—it is our duty and responsibility as Kingdom citizens.

REMEMBER, KINGDOM IS OUR FOCUS AND WE ARE JUST ONE IN A KINGDOM OF MANY!

It is a common practice in many of our churches for members to invest in their leaders, other members of the Body of Christ and those outside the church. This same practice must be a regular occurrence among our spiritual leaders. When God is using someone to build His Kingdom, leaders should want to get in on it. A leader's influence, resources, counsel and experience can help eliminate a lot of the unnecessary stress and strain attached to Kingdom ministry. It takes all of us working together, with a Kingdom focus, to get the job done. No one got to where they are by themself, someone helped them. Why not be that someone?In the end, the Kingdom benefits and God gets the glory!

IT IS OUR KINGDOM RESPONSIBILITY TO HELP OTHERS IN NEED!

"Let him that stole steal no more: but rather let him labor working with his hands the thing which is good, that he may have to give to him that needeth" (Ephesians 4:28). God wants to entrust us with millions to help those in need. One of the greatest prayers that we can pray outside of the prayer of salvation is to ask God to bless us to be a blessing to His people and the world. Our lives are to be testimonies for the Lord. God does not come down, He comes through us. He has placed His Holy Spirit on the inside of us to minister through us to the world.

We are God's agents in the world to do Kingdom business. So therefore, the more we have the more we can do for Him.The Bible says: **"But whoso hath this world's good, and seeth his brother have need, and shutteth up his bowels [heart] of compassion from him, how dwelleth the love of God in him" (1 John 3:17).** We exemplify the love of God to others by having compassion on them with our words and deeds (actions). **"My little children, let us not love in word, neither in tongue but in deed and in truth, and shall assure our hearts before him" (1 John 3:18).**

From our hearts proceeds the love of God to His people. We are to always monitor our hearts so that we can be used of God through Jesus Christ. We should never allow selfish ambitions to keep us from blessing God's people. If we should ever see our brothers and sisters in need and we have the means to help them, we should do so. God's word has revealed that this is how we should respond. We should not only love in words but in action as well. When someone has a Kingdom assignment on their lives and is walking in obedience to God's will, we should not miss the opportunity to be a blessing with our resources.

Millionaire Christians: Thinking and living beyond a paycheck, engagements and a prayer!

Chapter VI

Understanding Your Abilities For Kingdom Living

MOVING BEYOND THE PAYCHECK AND ENGAGEMENTS (HONORARIUMS)!

We were created to be people of ownership; remember, we have been blessed to dominate the earth. It is amazing that many individuals cannot see themselves living beyond a paycheck or a job. The mindset of some people is very limited, and they can only view their source of increase from a job in which they have allowed themselves to become solely dependent on. Now, it is good for us to work and make a living, but do not just limit your life to a job or an offering. For some people, the job will provide the resources or means that will bring them financial freedom by applying the principles of God's word. Remember, after you pay your tithes, the 90% that remains is blessed. Because this portion is already blessed, using it the right way will cause a great increase.

Living from paycheck to paycheck was not God's original plan for your life; you were created to be successful and prosperous, fruitful and flourishing. We were ordained and blessed to walk in wealth. This blessing was not taken away from us. However, over a period of time we began to lose focus of who we are, and have become what society says we are. Kingdom wealth is about gaining the understanding to remove all forms of bondage and an unhealthy dependency from our lives. It is possible to turn your situation around—to stop working for your money and let your money work for you.

Vision is necessary for us to tap into an unlimited source of financial increase in our lives. Without vision, we will never access all that God has for us. All great things start with an idea—the creation of the world first came out of the mind of God. We were also in the mind of God before He fashioned us. The bed we sleep in; the cars, buses and planes we use for travel; the house we live in; the types of communication we use; and the restaurants we eat in are all the result of an idea. This list can go on and on. But as we can see, all we need is a God-given idea.

The ability to dream is a wonderful gift, and this ability is necessary for financial increase. Without vision we will perish. We will always remain in a place where our money and resources are limited. However, when we dream, it now becomes a reality, and we now have the ability to move into a place of receiving unlimited resources and money. The Holy Spirit will speak through our visions and dreams; we must dream big to see big things happen. We must step out on faith and trust God to work the vision and dream. With God we can live a life of abundance for the rest our lives. If we understand the blessings of multiplication, replenishing, and fruitfulness that were bestowed upon us, we will be empowered to move into living a life of increase and financial prosperity.

Kingdom wealth is about prospering in every area of our life, and total prosperity is God's original plan for us. The Kingdom of God is about living the God-ordained life that was given to us by Him. I believe that believers of Jesus Christ are to be some of the most successful people who live in the earth. Our success is not based on the standards of the world but on the blessings of God on our lives; and God's blessings will always cause us to become the best.

God can give you ideas that will cause a great increase to come into your life. The Bible lets us know that God gives wisdom and witty inventions. **"I wisdom dwell with prudence, and find out knowledge of witty inventions" (Proverbs 8:12).** One God-given idea can make you financially healthy for the rest of your life. One idea from God plus the wisdom of the Holy Spirit can cause you to have financial success beyond what you can ever imagine.

DARE TO DREAM BEYOND WHERE YOU ARE AND SEE YOURSELF WHERE HE IS TRYING TO TAKE YOU!

The ideas that God gives to you will be from the giftings He has already put in you. God is the one who created you, and He already knows your capabilities and abilities. He is so wise that He never makes a mistake; nothing about how God made you is a mistake. Our choices can lead us to mistakes, but not God. You are not created to be like anyone else, so never judge yourself according to someone else, but focus on your original self. You flourish out of being you.

Being the best you is one of the greatest gifts that anyone can give to themselves. You can only flourish in your originality, not in becoming a carbon copy. When God made you, He only made one of you on purpose, for purpose and with purpose—every gift you have been given is for your purpose. Your gift was given to you to fulfill your destiny, which is the reason for which you were born. One of the keys to stepping into a place of financial prosperity is connecting your dreams with your gifts.

REMEMBER, YOUR GIFTS ARE YOURS; YOU OWN THEM AND NO ONE CAN TAKE THEM AWAY!

If you use the gift God has given you and allow yourself to dream big—bigger than where you are, bigger than where anyone has been—then you will tap into an unlimited stream of increase. You can never run out of your gift and you can never exhaust your gift; your gift comes out of you and is developed as you are developed. Therefore, you can never use your gift too much or run out of your gift as long as you live.

The greatest way to bring increase in your life is by using your gift; remember, you can never exhaust the gift God has given you, and one will never get tired of using their gift. Your passion comes out of your gift. If you don't know what your gift is, just pay attention to the things you do well and are passionate about. Your gift is what you do that is effortless. Others that do not have your gift will put forth a lot of effort to do it, but for you it is effortless. Your gift is not what you have been trained to do but what you naturally have the ability to do, and do well. However, despite having the natural ability, you should always find ways to enhance your gift. The ability that God was speaking about in Deuteronomy is the gift that He has given to you, because your gift is the ability to do what you do.

When you have multiple giftings, you then have multiple income streams locked up on the inside of you (many do not think about this), and to access your giftings you have to begin to use them. If you do not use your giftings then how can they bless you and do for you what they were designed to do. Even for the person who is walking and using their giftings, know that there is always another level on which you can use your gifts.

Visions and dreams will empower you to maximize your gifts. To reach the next level with your gifts you must be totally submitted to the Holy Spirit—there is no limit to your success in God. The gift alone can help you to have money, but true success is allowing the Holy Spirit to use your gifts to be a Kingdom builder. Now under stand, we all have a dominant gift which is our strongest ability, but we also have giftings that are not as strong, yet still can be profitable for us.

NOTE: ALL YOUR MINOR GIFTINGS WILL SUPPORT YOUR DOMINANT GIFT!

The key to finding your dominant gift and mastering it is by allowing the Holy Spirit to have control. Developing the true essence of who you are and have been created to be comes by allowing the Holy Spirit to develop your character. Godly character is our focus and we develop it by allowing the works of the flesh to die and the fruit of the Spirit to mature in us.

Your gifts have the ability to open doors for you, make relationships, put you on platforms, and allow the world to know your name and who you are. But your character is needed to maintain your success. God is always more pleased with your character than the expression of your gift. Gifts are not very effective if integrity and godly character is missing. Allowing the fruit of the Spirit to mature in your life is how the Holy Spirit helps to build your character. When you have godly character, the anointing on your life will increase and saturate your gifts, and this will cause increase and flourishing in your life. Your character reveals your true self. This comes from the state of a man's heart: clean hands and a pure heart is what God desires of us. Please understand that whatever is in your heart will come out.

> **O generation of vipers, how can ye, being evil, speak good things? for out of the abundance of the heart the mouth speaketh. A good man out of the good**

treasure of the heart bringeth forth good things: and an evil man out of the evil treasure bringeth forth evil things. (Matthew 12:34-35)

When some level of success is achieved it will always cause that which is dormant in a person to manifest. This is why we have so many in the Body of Christ throughout the ages who started out good but ended poorly. The key to your success in God is to end stronger than how you began.The process of God in building godly character in you is designed to purify you, not destroy you. Let the character of Christ grow in you by living according to His guidance, the instructions of the Holy Spirit, the commandments and the wisdom of the scriptures.

So now, how do you move beyond a paycheck and a speaking engagement? By using gifts that God has given to you. Moving beyond the speaking engagement means you are not waiting on someone to call you to preach to meet your needs, but using everything God has given you to produce and multiply your resources. The platforms He gives you to speak on should never be about money, but about souls and the will of God. There are too many ministers who find themselves staying so focused on an engagement and not the assignment. Some have become more concerned about honorariums and not the assignment, which is to build and establish the Kingdom.

Now I believe that all ministers of the Gospel are worthy to receive the best offering that a ministry can afford to give; there is no amount too large that one can receive for bringing a message of hope, salvation, healing and deliverance to the people of God. The greater the demands on your life, the greater the needs; so of course it is necessary for us to receive the best love offering possible. Jesus was not a poor man despite many opinions. A poor man would not need a treasurer to handle His money. So the amount is not the issue, it is the focus. We should never compromise the integrity of God's word just for a large offering; we are called to preach the Gospel and the word of God, not our opinions. We are ministers of the Kingdom of God and God wants us to have everything we need to do what He called us to do.

Why did I say we must also move beyond a prayer? Notice I said beyond a prayer and not a lifestyle of prayer. We need to move beyond praying to God only when we are stressed out and need money. Many of us only pray for money when we have none or are running out, or when we have bills to pay and there is not enough money to pay them. When we have needs that require money, and our funds are insufficient, this is when some of us become diligent in prayer.

I believe that if many of us really had all the money we wanted, we perhaps would never pray—or pray very little. Lack of money keeps many of us on our knees. Simply praying and asking God for money will not result in a permanent change of your financial status, but asking the Lord to show you how to use what He has given you to earn money will bring a great and permanent change in your finances. Even those who have money and want more money pray more about what they want instead of praying for the will of God to be done with what they already have.

Kingdom wealth is not about praying a prayer just for today's needs, but it is about praying for everything we need to do Kingdom work, praying to have so we can give away and praying to have so we can be a blessing to others. Kingdom-driven prayer is more about the will of God for our lives instead of our desire for things. When we pray, we must be very sensitive to God's instructions. He instructs us to follow Him, not to ignore what He says.

Following the instruction and guidance of the Holy Spirit is crucial to achieving the increase necessary to move beyond a speaking engagement, a paycheck and a prayer.

Prayer was not given to us to beg God for money; it was given to us to commune, fellowship and communicate with God. Asking God to supply our needs is great, but how He does this is where we miss it. It is very rare that we will just stumble upon money, or that someone will call us and sow millions of dollars into our lives. Even though this is not impossible, it is not likely to happen.

So many of our prayers consist of asking God to give us money but rarely asking God for more of Himself. With more of God we will have the power to produce more of what we need. Kingdom wealth requires us to seek God for our relationship to go to another dimension in Him which will, in turn, bring us into a place of total prosperity. Yes, we are always to seek the Lord for direction concerning our businesses and finances.

Yes, God wants to be involved in our daily decisions and He wants to supply our daily bread and needs. However, we will experience this automatically if we focus on our relationship with Him, and worship and praise Him at all times. God's response time to our situations is quicker when we praise and worship Him, ask Him to provide and allow Him to guide us into our wealthy place He has originally purposed for us.

Take the limits off of yourself by removing fear, doubt and insecurity; pray for wisdom and understanding of who you are and how you are ordained to live. You can have all that God has for you, but first you must recognize it and then access it. Freedom from personal fears is necessary in acquiring the wealth of the Kingdom for your life. See yourself as God sees you, not as men see you. Men say you cannot have that, you cannot do this. God's word says it best: **"I can do all things through Christ which strengtheneth me" (Philippians 4:12).** There are no limits to the money you can have; the only limit is the one you put on yourself.

How do we get money? By using wisely our 90% that God allows us to have, by using the gifts that God has given to us, by allowing our gifts to make room for us and by following His instructions. Allow the Spirit of thc Lord to open doors to ministering the message of His Kingdom. Doing your Kingdom assignment brings the guarantee that God will take care of you. How you earn and spend your money determines a lot about you, and it sends a message to others about how you see yourself.

The Bible tells us that money "answereth all things," so yes, part of Kingdom wealth is having money. **"A feast is made for laughter, and wine maketh merry: but money answereth all things" (Ecclesiastes 10:19).** It is important to have money, but how we get the money is the issue. Your gift is designed to bring you increase, favor, open doors and, of course, money. We see how the gifts of so many people are allowing them to make millions around the globe; there is a connection between your gift, your character and your money.

Now some might not want to see it this way, but just turn on your television or go to the malls, and you will see how millions of people are using their gifts—and their gifts are bringing them money. However, for Kingdom citizens, our gifts cannot just bring us money but they must be used to glorify God first, and then the money will come. As a Kingdom citizen, you should not just strive to use your gifts, but also submit your gifts to God so He can put His supernatural on your natural. Let Him smear the anointing on you and your gifts. Gifts without the anointing can bring you money, but gifts that are anointed will bring you Kingdom wealth.

THE LOVE OF MONEY IS THE ROOT OF ALL EVIL—YOU CANNOT LOVE MONEY SO MUCH THAT IT BECOMES YOUR DRIVING FORCE IN LIFE!

The minute you love money more than your Kingdom assignment is the day you've crossed into a place of danger, which will open you up to become compromised and corrupt. Remember that once you pay your tithes and regular offering, the 90% is blessed; and because it is already blessed, what you do with it will bring you back an increase in whatever area you invest. Now this is important—you must be careful what you do with this portion of money. It is not about how much you have, but what you do with what you have that makes the difference.

Understand that many of you have different amounts to work with; however, the amount is not the issue. Again I say, what you do with it is the issue. You cannot take blessed money and use it on ungodly things—God will only allow the blessing to flow when the money is used in a godly way. So now we have to talk about the way in which we invest the blessed portion so that it will bring us to the Kingdom wealth status intended by God.

Step I

A. To be effective with the 90%, you must respect money. Respecting money will allow you to make wise decisions with it. Money will come to you when you make key decisions about how to save, spend and invest.

B. It is important for you to show your maturity by how you spend your money. (One can always tell the level of understanding and maturity a person has by how they spend their time and money.)

C. You must budget, invest and save your money. Our money will increase when we allow it to work for us. Use your money to invest in yourself as well as others. You do not have to wait to have a large sum of money to begin investing and saving. Invest at the level that you are at, and as your money increases your savings and investments will also increase.

Investing your money is one of the ways you allow your money to work for you, and you not work for it. If you do not know how to start, pray and ask the Holy Spirit to lead you—He is the best banker and broker I know. Ministers, strive to do things in a spirit of excellence. Do things that will enhance your ministry and prepare you for where you are going, not where you are. There is nothing wrong with getting a return on your money—remember, we have been blessed to multiply.

Step II

Money can only be used in three ways. It can be used to: 1) save and invest, 2) spend, and 3) give away! Remember, how you spend your money shows where you are. Get the understanding of God's view of wealth and not the world's view. There is nothing wrong with making money as long as we do not violate the word of God to make it.

The anointing of prosperity will deliver you from debt and poverty. The Bible says, **"And the yoke shall be destroyed because of the anointing" (Isaiah 10:27b).** Therefore, the yoke of poverty needs the anointing of prosperity. Connect with the anointing of prosperity, invest and sow, and watch the anointing begin to flow in your life. As Kingdom citizens, our focus is not just on money but wealth. As Kingdom citizens, our focus is not on self-gratification but glorifying God. As Kingdom citizens, our focus is not on fruitless works but fruitful works. As Kingdom citizens, we must tap into our dominant gift, master it, submit to the Holy Spirit and develop our godly character—then we can expect an increase. Our focus is always on building the Kingdom of God, not the kingdom of man.

PROPHESY TO GOD'S PEOPLE ABOUT WHO WE ARE IN GOD AND WHAT HE HAS IMPARTED INTO US!

Chapter VII

Accessing a Kingdom Lifestyle of Wealth

HAVING MONEY DOES NOT MEAN YOU ARE WEALTHY!

Kingdom wealth is all about prosperity in every area of our lives. The next area of prosperity pertaining to Kingdom wealth is our souls. Kingdom wealth is more than money because you can be rich and still not be wealthy. An impoverished mind leads to an impoverished soul, an impoverished soul leads to an impoverished spirit and an impoverished spirit leads to an impoverished life!

If being wealthy was all about having money, then many rich people would not commit suicide, be on drugs or alcohol, live a life full of lust and addictions, and so much more. These types of behaviors are linked to a root cause in our soul: some type of depravity or lack that may have come as a result of never receiving what we needed as children or adults. Many of us have experienced some type of hurt, disappointment, rejection, insecurity, low-self esteem or abandonment that has left us with unresolved issues in our soul.

The root causes of pain in our soul is a result of several reasons: emotional needs that were never met, or emotional issues that were never healed or resolved. Remember, we all have, in some way, become a product of or have been affected by our environment, life situations and circumstances. Without proper understanding and healing of these issues, we can go through life and never really understand why we are so broken, hurt or feel such bondage. The wealth of our soul manifests when we become free from these issues and root causes that have kept us in bondage emotionally. Emotional wealth can be one of the most difficult things to experience due to many of us not being transparent enough about our emotional state. For some of us, it is easier to make millions than it is for us to deal with our emotions.

Prosperity of the soul is essential for us to enjoy all the other areas of prosperity in our life. Our soul is the most dominant and controlling part of our being; however, through salvation and obedience to God's word, we can have the wealth God intended for us in our soul. One of the keys to achieving soul prosperity is overcoming the flesh by allowing the fruit of the Spirit to mature in our lives. A healthy mind equals a healthy soul, which leads to an empowered spirit. This then results in a wealthy life—the God-ordained life.

Kingdom wealth is about having freedom in every area of your life—soul, body (money) and spirit. It is very good to have money, but money is only valuable in the natural realm. Money can only get you material things and natural opportunities, but only the Spirit of God can get you spiritual abundance and new life in the Spirit. God does require us to use our natural resources to support Kingdom work; however, we cannot do Kingdom work effectively if we are in emotional bondage.

We are the makeup of our soul, body and spirit; the human makeup is so tightly interwoven that each part of us affects the other. Therefore, understanding how God wants us to live and then living this way will bring us into our wealthy place in Him. Let's start by looking at what God requires of us.

God does want us to be rich, but He also wants us to live holy. Holiness is not a request but a command: **"Because it is written, BE YE HOLY; for I am HOLY" (1 Peter 1:16, *emphasis author's*).** Holiness cannot be achieved by what you do, but by what you allow Christ to do in you. The Jewish people tried to uphold the Law of Moses to the letter and still were unable to attain the level of holiness God required of them. If they could not keep the Law outside of Christ, what makes us think we can? Jesus is the righteousness of God that is imputed unto us.

This does not mean we can do anything we want to do and say—because of Jesus we are Holy. We still must practice self-control and abstain from immoral behavior. We, through Christ, have the ability to do that. The power of the Holy Spirit is the one who keeps us and helps us to live holy. Holiness is Christ in us coupled with living according to the instructions of the Word. Christ is the one who was sent into the world to keep, convict and prompt us to repent if we sin. Determination and right decision-making is vital to living a life of holiness before the Lord.

Holiness is also a part of being wealthy. Holiness keeps your soul (will, mind, emotions, desires, intellect) and body healthy, and your spirit empowered. We as Kingdom citizens are called to live a sanctified life—to be set apart from the world. But many times we do not hear about God's standard for living. Holiness is God's standard by which we are to live. To receive all the benefits from the Kingdom, you must be connected to the King who owns the Kingdom. The enemy did not and still does not know all that God has in store for us; but he knows enough that if he can keep us disconnected from God, then he will hinder us from receiving our God-given inheritance. Holiness is a prerequisite to us receiving and living in the fullness of the wealth that God has for us.

When we live a life of holiness, we are separated from the works of the flesh. The works of the flesh lead to a poverty-stricken life. All works of the flesh lead to a form of depravity in our souls and a disconnection in our spirits. It is God's intention for our souls to prosper and be in health. The works of the flesh cause issues and strongholds (or root causes that are internal), and practicing these types of behaviors cause bondage and lack. All works of the flesh are destructive to our human soul in many ways.

As stated earlier, the works of the flesh lead to poverty, lack and depravity in our soul. A soul that is full of works of the flesh is a soul that is unhealthy. Remember, a healthy soul is a prosperous soul. Let us look at what these behaviors are, and at the damage they cause when allowed to manifest in our lives.

The Works of the Flesh

- **I.** **Adultery**—sexual immorality, sexual intercourse between a married person and someone to whom that person is not married to
- **II.** **Fornication**—intercourse between two unmarried persons
- **III.** **Uncleanness**—sexual impurity, impure thoughts, homosexuality (sexual intercourse between persons of the same sex)
- **IV.** **Lasciviousness**—lust, sexual excess, eagerness for lustful pleasure
- **V.** **Idolatry**—not just the worship of graven images, but also putting one's chief affections on any object or person instead of on God
- **VI.** **Witchcraft**—sorcery; tampering with powers of evil, participating in demonic activities, which also includes dabbling in the occult

VII. **Hatred**—hostility
VIII. **Variance**—strife or discord, quarreling, lying
IX. **Emulations**—jealousy
X. **Wrath**—outbursts of anger
XI. **Strife**—selfish ambition (self-centered, self-seeking desire for achievement of power, fame, wealth, etc.; greedy, self-absorbed and only doing things for personal gain)
XII. **Seditions**—dissensions
XIII. **Heresies**—a permanent, organized division or clique (the feeling that everyone is wrong except for their own little groups)
XIV. **Envying**—envy
XV. **Murders**
XVI. **Drunkenness**
XVII **Reveling**—excessive eating, gluttony or carousing, wild living

> **Of the which I tell you before, as I have also told you in time past, that they which do such things shall not inherit the kingdom of God. (Galatians 5:21b)**

> **Know ye not that the unrighteous shall not inherit the Kingdom of God? Be not deceived: neither fornicators, nor idolaters, nor adulterers, nor effeminate, nor abusers of themselves with mankind. Nor thieves, nor covetous, nor drunkards, nor revilers, nor extortioners, shall inherit the kingdom of God. (1 Corinthians 6:9-10)**

Allowing these wrong desires, works of the flesh and actions to enter our lives will lead to destruction, lack, depravation and death. Our wrong desires are evil, destructive, easy to ignite, difficult to stifle and even tougher to stop. They are self-centered, oppressive and possessive, decadent, sinful and deadly. These things are not to be named among the believers. When the Bible speaks of working out your soul salvation, these are the things it is referring to. We need the Holy Spirit to dig up out of our soul every destructive, selfish work.

No amount of money can get you delivered from the works of the flesh—it takes the power of God to set you free and keep you free. If we have these desires in our life, and money, money will only open up more options for us to express and operate in these destructive behaviors. The works of the flesh are an enemy to our spirit and soul. We are not supposed to sleep with or entertain the enemy, but we are to resist the enemy. These fleshly desires must be resisted so they can flee from our soul.

The works of the flesh will keep you out of the Kingdom as well, and hinder you from obtaining your Kingdom rights and benefits. All these works will keep you in bondage and will not allow you to inherit the Kingdom of God. Bondage of any kind is not of God, and soul bondage is a hindrance to obtaining the prosperity of God and experiencing the fullness of the Kingdom in your life. Being set apart from all the works of the flesh will help us to live holy. Being holy is simply living the way God has commanded us to live—free from the works of the flesh.

As Christians, we are required to live a holy life that reflects the nature of God. We are to separate ourselves from the actions, influences and people that will contaminate us. We must apply the biblical standard of purity and holiness, and avoid what is unholy and against God's standard of righteousness. Righteousness is God's standard of living. The Kingdom of God is not meat and drink, meaning it is not rules and regulations of the world, but the standard of God.

Through Jesus Christ, righteousness was imputed into our spirit and is now manifesting in our soul. Righteousness manifests in our life when our desires, will, emotions and character change. We will not desire the same things we did before we were saved—our lifestyle should never harm our bodies or allow other offenses to the Holy Spirit.

So we understand that an unholy lifestyle starts in our minds and then results in our actions. Poverty of the mind is a result of the works of the flesh and can be overcome by living a life that is pleasing to God. This type of mindset hinders us from acquiring the wealth of God and puts us in a place of idolatry and strife. **"Wherefore come out from among them, and be ye separate, saith the Lord, and touch not the unclean thing; and I will receive you" (2 Corinthians 6:17).**

YOU ARE NOT WEALTHY IN GOD IF YOU ARE LIVING UNHOLY!

And so we now understand that a poverty mindset or an unholy mindset is of the world. It sees the world as its source and not God. This mindset keeps you in bondage. When a person has a poverty mindset, they can live in a palace but act like a pauper. This comes from not understanding the lifestyle God requires in order to be wealthy.

"AS A MAN THINKETH IN HIS HEART SO IS HE." PROVERBS 23:7B

A person that has a poverty mindset thinks only about today, but a wealthy person thinks beyond today; they think years, not days ahead. A wealthy person thinks about more than themselves; they think about the lives of others and how they can help.

I remember some years ago watching a television show where an experiment was being conducted on people who quickly came into large sums of money. The results of this research were astounding: there were individuals who won millions in the lottery, but just a few years later they were broke. There were individuals who won lawsuits, and in a few months were penniless. Some, in fact, were in worse shape after the money was gone than before they received the money.

On this particular show, they took a man off the streets and gave him thousands of dollars. They followed his life after he received the money. The results were that in just a short space of time, this man ended up right back where he started—in the streets. Why? Because he did not have the proper mindset to handle his money nor the spiritual readiness for wealth. He had the money but did not know how to properly spend it to make a better life for himself.

Wealth does not come from getting rich quick; however, true wealth starts in your spirit and then in your mind. The manifestation then shows up in your life. If the manifestation comes before the preparation, it will not last. God's system of increase is that manifestation follows preparation. Kingdom wealth is about allowing your soul to be healed, and your mind and spirit to be empowered to walk in your rightful place in the Kingdom.

Your spirit and soul must be ready for wealth in order for you to become totally wealthy. Wealth starts in your spirit, changes your soul and then manifests in your life. **"But the fruit of the Spirit is love, joy, peace, longsuffering, gentleness, goodness, faith, meekness, temperance: against such there is no law" (Galatians 5:22-23).** Allowing the fruit of the Spirit in your life to mature will cause you to flourish and become healthy in every area. Remember, God wants our spirits, souls, bodies and finances to be wealthy.

In order to become spiritually wealthy, we must live a life that is pleasing to God—a life of holiness, prayer, fasting, reading, studying the Word and being a true worshiper. Live a life of daily praise unto God. These are our daily requirements from God. Having the Fruit in your life will always keep you free from every work of the flesh and empower you to live in your abundant life. A wealthy soul is achieved when we allow the fruit of the Spirit to mature in our lives. Here are the essential ingredients to maintaining a healthy soul.

I. **Love**—the willing, sacrificial giving of oneself for the benefit of another without thought of return

II. **Joy**—gladness of heart

III. **Peace**—tranquility of mind freeing one from worry and fear

IV. **Longsuffering**—patience with others, the opposite of a short temper, a disposition quietly bearing injury

V. **Gentleness**—kindness

VI. **Goodness**—generosity (to everyone, not just to the individuals that are nice to you)

VII. **Faith**—dependability, being unconsciously and consciously dependent on God

VIII. **Meekness**—gentleness, that is, courtesy and consideration of one's relations with others

IX. **Temperance**—self-control, that is the ability to harness and control one's passions and lusts

When the fruit of the Spirit is manifesting in our lives we are good, productive, self-giving, liberating, uplifting, and holy, which leads us to an abundant life. When the Fruit is in us, the works of the flesh are difficult to ignite and easy to stifle. The war that goes on within us is with the works of the flesh versus living with the fruit of the Spirit. We must do what the Bible says and allow our flesh to die daily.

There are some things that are easy for us to let die, but there are others that are more difficult. Therefore, you find yourself in a state of unproductiveness, stagnation and fear. Stubbornness to godly change does not benefit you, it only keeps you in a state of lack and destruction longer. The longer it takes for you to submit to the Holy Spirit for change, the more unproductive you will become. There are individuals who appear to be doing well; however, if the works of the flesh are still in them, they are still not living in the fullness of what God has.

There is no compromising when living with the works of the flesh. God is not a compromising God—you have to do it God's way to receive all that He has for you. We cannot be successful in God if we continue to allow the works of the flesh to be the ruling force in our lives. These fleshly desires are what were birthed in our soul when Adam sinned and man became a dying soul. Christ came to bring back full restoration of the spirit and healing to the souls of mankind.

All of the Fruit, when allowed to mature in our lives, will enable us to be free from the lack and bondage of the enemy, and maintain our divine wealth that comes from God through salvation and the administration of the Holy Spirit. True wealth comes from your spirit through Christ into your soul, then into your life. A wealthy life is a life of abundance that comes from God and God alone. True wealth is total prosperity of man God's way—in every area: soul, spirit and body.

LIMITED THINKING "VERSUS" LIMITLESS THINKING! BEING RICH "VERSUS" BEING WEALTHY!

A wealthy person is not limited in their thinking, but a rich person is. Riches are a part of being wealthy, but they are not the totality of it. True wealth comes from following the instructions of God. If you give Jesus Christ first precedence in your life, He will give you instructions on how to experience all that God has for you. Jesus is Lord of our lives and without Him, we cannot experience the full harvest He has for us. In our ministries, homes, businesses, and jobs, Jesus wants to be the focus. Putting Jesus first will allow the Holy Spirit to lead and guide us into all truth and abundance.

The world's system of wealth is all about how much money you have, but God's system of wealth is about first our lifestyle of righteousness, favor, and then the money. **"But seek ye first the kingdom of God, and his righteousness; and all these things shall be added unto you" (Matthew 6:33).** Seeking the Kingdom of God and His righteousness should exceed your pursuit of riches and things. God wants us to have the things we need to live a prosperous life, but they should not be our sole desire. I believe we are to enjoy the world and everything in it, but it should not be done outside the will of God. It is the will of God for us to have everything we need in every area of our lives, but God wants us to not just have things, He wants us to put Him first; this is living the Kingdom life.

God's favor is necessary to experience God's Kingdom wealth. Favor can cause increase to come into your life, when money is not necessary. Favor can get you what money cannot. Many of you have been asking God for money, but favor brings you money. You can be a billionaire and still not be wealthy. If your spirit is bankrupt, your soul is in bondage. True Kingdom wealth brings liberty in every area of your life.

With Kingdom wealth also comes the responsibilities for us to live the right way. True Kingdom wealth is not just for us to live a great life and have a healthy soul, an empowered spirit, great material things, and a wonderful relationship, and then never share. It is to empower everyone else to gain the same knowledge and understanding so they can access and experience this God-ordained life themselves. It is to be used to bring others into their Kingdom wealth as well. It is to help others understand what it means to be wealthy in the Kingdom and use their resources to build the Kingdom of God. Money is a part of wealth; however, money is not given to you for you not to share.

To maintain your Kingdom finances, you have to share so you can continue to replenish and multiply. The blessings of replenishing cannot make you full or complete again and again if nothing ever goes out. Remember, the **Five Principles of Success** are to be fruitful, multiply, replenish, subdue and have dominion. This will not work effectively if you are not willing to use it to expand God's Kingdom.

ACCESSING OUR GOD-ORDAINED KINGDOM WEALTH REQUIRES A LIFESTYLE OF CHANGE AND OBEDIENCE!!

Chapter VIII

Experiencing Kingdom Abundance

PREPARATION FOR THE WEALTH REQUIREMENTS!

Step I—Self Change

Change is defined as to become different or to make different, a transformation or modification.

As human beings, change is one of the most difficult tasks. Change is not easy, but it is very necessary. Change requires self-effort as well as divine intervention. In order for individuals to change, they must see a need, as well as a desire for change. No one can change you but you and God. God does not force us to change; He does, however, show us the need for change and gives us the tools and information needed to help us change.

Many people spend their lives trying to change others, but can I submit to you that this is wasted effort. We cannot change anyone, but we can be the agents to help individuals see and understand the need for change. God gave us a will, and He will not force us to change beyond our will. God will show us the need to be different, then it is up to us to apply the information in our lives so that change can take place. Change is a result of our effort, enabled and sustained by divine support and help.

There is a saying that I have always heard: "If you want what you've never had you must do what you've never done." Understanding how our minds work will enable us to begin the process of change. There are many of us who spend years doing the same thing, never understanding that our behavior is the hindrance to obtaining the abundance of God's wealth in our lives. Experiencing Kingdom wealth requires us to think, act and be different. The first step to change is to understand how powerful our thoughts are.

A. Thoughts—Everything begins with a thought. Before God created us, we understood that according to the scripture, He first had a thought. Following the thought of God, His word spoke us into existence, and then His actions began the creative process. Then God created man in His image and likeness.

It is important to understand that our thoughts shape our destiny. The Bible says: **"For as he thinketh in his heart, so is he" (Proverbs 23:7a).** What we think is very crucial to who we become! The word of God says:

> **Finally, brethren, whatsoever things are true, whatsoever things are honest, whatsoever things are just, whatsoever things are pure, whatsoever things are lovely, whatsoever things are of good report, if there be any virtue, and if there be any praise, think on these things.**
>
> **(Philippians 4:8)**

Our thoughts must be aligned with God's word; it is very important for us to think scripturally about our lives. Every facet of our lives requires us to think according to God's word. This is the only way we can achieve a successful and complete victory in our thoughts.

This is a crucial step to accessing and experiencing the abundant life. Our thoughts then lead to the next step.

B. Words—Our words contain the power of life and death. Our words have creative force behind them. As believers in the Kingdom of God, we must be careful what we speak. Our world is shaped and framed by the words of our mouth.

"Death and life are in the power of the tongue: and they that love it shall eat the fruit thereof" (Proverbs 18:21). Our words move things in the realm of the Spirit, so we must be careful what we say. When we pray and rebuke the enemy, it is done by using the word of God. When we resist the enemy, it is done with our words and actions. When we worship and praise God, we use our words, actions, thoughts, decisions and character. Words are one of the most important attributes we have as believers; and how we use them can release blessings in our lives, or curses. Worship comes out of who we are—this determines what we do, say and think.

Words are one of the most powerful forces we have in the universe to frame our life and destiny. We will have and become what we say. Words activate the power of creation. Every word has the ability to be productive or destructive. It is important and necessary for every Kingdom believer to speak the language of the Kingdom! We not only have citizenship, rights, benefits and privileges, but we also have a language.

The Kingdom language consists solely of the word of God. The Spirit realm responds to our Kingdom language. All other languages are foreign and will not release our blessings or bring Kingdom results. Everything in the universe, both seen (natural) and unseen (spiritual), responds to God's words. We have been given God's word, which is Kingdom language. Through the indwelling presence of the Holy Spirit, we live in our Kingdom abundance. Begin today to commit to speaking only your Kingdom language by canceling and pulling out of the atmosphere every negative word, and by canceling every negative thought.

Pray This Prayer

Father God in the name of Jesus, I thank you for opening the eyes of my understanding to see the power of my words and thoughts. In the name of Jesus, I cancel every negative word and word curse that has been spoken out of my mouth and over my life. I pull down every vain and false imagination that exalts itself against the knowledge of God. I speak to my mind and I say let this mind be in me which was in Christ Jesus. I now ask you, Holy Spirit, to touch my mind so I can think and speak according to the word of God.

Thank you, Father, for helping me to think on that which is lovely, that which is true, that which is just, that is which is powerful, so there can be virtue and praise. I thank you that because of your Word, God, and the power of the Holy Spirit, my mind and words are now in agreement with your words. Thank you for knowledge and understanding. Thank you that I am no longer destroying my destiny with my mouth. I thank you that I am what the Word says I am—I can do what the Word says I can do. My feet are set on God's ordained course for my life. I am victorious, and from this day forward my language has become Kingdom language. I bless you Father and praise you. In Jesus' name. Amen.

Now begin to speak the word of God. This will now set in motion your wealth and release the abundance in your life. Our thoughts lead to our words, which lead to our decisions.

C. Decisions—What we think and speak is what determines our decisions.

Wrong thoughts lead to wrong words which lead to bad or wrong decisions. One of the greatest abilities that God has given to us is the power of choice. We are not robots in God's hand, we are free agents with the ability of choice. God does not choose for us, but the Holy Spirit does and will aid us with everything we need to make godly choices. Joshua said to the people of Israel:

> **And if it seem evil unto you to serve the Lord, choose you this day whom ye will serve; whether the gods which your fathers served that were on the other side of the flood, or the gods of the Amorites, in whose land ye dwell: but as for me and my house, we will serve the Lord.**
>
> **(Joshua 24:15)**

Joshua understood that the people had a choice to either serve God or not! He knew that he could not force them, but it was clear that Joshua's choice was that he and his household were going to serve the Lord. You see, self-change is the same way: one cannot force you to change, you must make the decision and declaration that you are going to change and serve the Lord.

If we just take a moment and reflect on our lives, we will see that our lives are a sum total of our decisions—good or bad. Our decision to do or not to do have led us to this point. In life we only have two choices: to serve God or the devil, good or evil, right or wrong. And for us to change, we must make the choice. However, we do have a lot of options of how we can exercise the choices we make.

Now as believers, you may be saying that you are saved and not serving the enemy. If the decisions that you are making are not in line with the word of God and His requirements, then whom are you serving? God requires us to give Him glory out of our lives by what we say, do and become. No man can serve two masters. The Bible says that we must serve one and hate the other. We cannot justify doing wrong by saying, "God knows my heart."

God has given us everything we need to serve Him in truth and righteousness. Allowing yourself to change means, "I am going to let my old character go and allow the character of Christ to develop in me daily." When we become saved, our spirit is regenerated but our soul still needs a lot of work. Our will, mind, desires, emotions, thoughts and actions must line up with the fruit of the Spirit.

Each of you reading this book will find yourself in a different place in life. But one thing is true, all of you have made some type of decision that led you to this point. As long as we live in this flesh we will always have areas in our lives that need to change. We were born with this nature because of sin, but because of salvation we are becoming like Christ.

When we came to Christ we began a new life and became a new person: old things now are passed away and our new nature is evolving. Now understand that this is a constant process of change. Salvation was instantaneous the moment you repented, confessed and accepted Christ. The character development of Christ, however, is a lifelong process. Our thoughts lead to our words; our words lead to our decisions; our decisions lead to our actions.

D. Actions—Actions are defined as the process of doing.

What we think is often time what we do. It is very difficult for us to separate our decisions from our actions. We can tell what decisions a person has made based on their actions. Wrong actions can have devastating effects. So many individuals today find themselves having a very difficult time because of their actions. Our actions come as a result of our thoughts, words and decisions. The mind has a formula on how it connects our thoughts to our words—to our decisions—which in turn manifest in our actions.

It is very important that we keep our mind healthy because it is the controlling force in who we become. The desires of a person's heart are automatically connected to their thought process; this is why it is important for our hearts to be filled with the word of God and not the desires of the flesh. The process of becoming is somewhat complex, that's why the process of change is equally complex. Therefore, it is important to understand the formula of the mind in order to achieve change.

In God we first receive the Word in our spirit. The Word is then processed in our mind, spoken out of our mouth and then acted upon. Therefore, personal change must first begin in our spirit. The Apostle Paul helped us to know and understand that we still have to work daily on our soul. (Philippians 2:12) Thinking, speaking and decision-making must all be aligned with our actions. For this reason, you cannot say one thing and do the opposite, because what you do is more powerful than what you say. **"And whatsoever we ask, we receive of him, because we keep his commandments, and do those things that are pleasing in his sight" (1 John 3:22).**

LACK OF GODLY DECISIONS LEADS TO INADEQUATE OR BAD ACTIONS!

Our thoughts lead to our words, our words lead to our decisions, our decisions lead to our actions, our actions lead to our habits.

E. Habits—Habit is defined as an acquired behavior pattern regularly followed until it has become almost involuntary. A person's continuous actions are what form a habit.

Bad habits lead to bad results. If we continue to eat the wrong food, we can have serious problems with our physical health. If we misdirect our mind, emotions, will, and desires, we will have problems within our soul. If we do not pray, fast, live holy, study and apply the word of God to our life, we will have problems in our spirit. Every bad habit leads to serious problems that have equally serious consequences. However, godly habits lead to a healthy, wealthy, prosperous life in our soul, body and spirit.

Bad habits did not just start as habits, they started as thoughts. Good, godly habits are not just going to come to us, they must come from our thoughts, to our words, and then to our decisions. They will ultimately manifest in our actions continuously and repeatedly. At this point, we need to do a self-examination of who we are, what we do and how we have become. Then speak the change that you want to see and make the decision to become that change.

Our thoughts lead to our words, our words lead to our decisions, our decisions lead to our actions, our actions lead to our habits and our habits leads to our character. Our character is linked to our lifestyle. How we live is directly related to who we are.

F. Character—The sum total of features and traits that form the individual nature of a person, with reference to behavior or personality.

Our character is the sum total of our habits, which is directly connected to who we are and what we do. Understanding the journey to our thoughts, to our habits and to our character gives us a better understanding of the process that enables us to change. Change is not easy, but it is very attainable.

All behavior has a root cause, and for us to be free from a behavior or habit, we must deal with the root cause of that behavior. Dealing with the root cause of a behavior is one of the keys for that behavior to go away. A behavior will not go away if we just focus on the behavior; instead we must go beyond the behavior to its source. If the source or root cause for why we have the behavior is not dealt with, the behavior will come back and surface over and over again until it is dealt with.

As discussed above, the thoughts which end up in our character are essential for the process of change. The root cause is directly linked to the thoughts, words, actions and habits of a person. If we understanding that all behaviors have a source or root cause, just trying to stop the behavior will only result in temporary change. The goal is to achieve permanent change. To achieve permanent change we must allow the Holy Spirit to work in us, on us, with us and through us. Attaining the character of Jesus Christ is our goal.

To access and experience the wealth of the Kingdom of God, we must allow Him to rule our lives by the power of His Spirit, and then and only then will the true, God-ordained life be manifested in us. There is always a reason why we do what we do. For many of us, the reason is not easily known or discovered, but by being truthful to ourselves, and allowing the Holy Spirit to search to our soul, we will find the answer to why we have such behaviors.

There are numerous reasons why we do what we do, and yes, sin usually is at the base of the reason. We live in a sinful world and sinful things happen; however, that does not excuse us from doing a self-assessment to find the core reason for our negative behavior. I will discuss this topic more in my next book, *Kingdom Worshipers*. Let us now look at a few helpful tools to get you started. To find the root cause of one behavior we must always ask the question, "Why?" "Why am I doing what I am doing?" "Why am I the way I am?" "Why do I feel the way I feel?" "Why does this situation always seem to happen to me?" "Why do I attract certain types of people?" Asking the "Why" question is the first step that will help you begin to discover the issues beneath the behaviors that have hindered your change.

The Holy Spirit is the greatest agent given to us to aid in the process of change. Remember, the Holy Spirit is our helper, comforter, teacher, counselor and guide. The Holy Spirit is the power of God in the earth. This means that if we cooperate with Him, not only will He help facilitate our change, but He will help us sustain our change. No one is exempt from this process because no matter who we are and how long we have been living and serving God, we still have areas in our lives that we need to change. Paul made a great declaration to us when he said, **"Wherefore, my beloved, as ye have always obeyed, not as in my presence only, but now as in my absence, work out your own salvation with fear and trembling" (Philippians 2:12).**

This is a constant process and not a onetime event. It is necessary for us to always do a truthful self-examination. The fruit of the Spirit must mature in our lives for our change. Constant, truthful examination of ourselves will help us to keep the prosperity of our soul. The Apostle John, in his third letter, states: **"Beloved, I wish above all things that thou mayest prosper and be in health, even as thy soul prospereth" (3 John 2).** There are things we must do to enhance our soul, such as rid our mind, will, emotions and intellect of the desires and thoughts that are not of God. Change is necessary for our soul to prosper and to access the wealth God has for us.

Step II—Self Development

We must continue to develop ourselves every day. Self-development is an ongoing process that must be intentional and purposeful. In self-development, we must set goals for ourselves and reach them. Our spiritual goals consist of increasing our prayer and study time, and developing a life of fasting and consecration. Goals for our soul will consist of riding our mind of negative thoughts. Our goals for our body will consist of eliminating certain foods from our diet, exercising more regularly and increasing our knowledge on health and nutrition. Self-development requires you to improve yourself. In the self-examining process, which should be done daily, look for things to improve about yourself. This exercise will always keep you growing and becoming better.

In self-development, learn your strengths and weaknesses—learn the strength of your gifts and master them. Subdue and conquer your weaknesses; and develop you minor giftings so you can be balanced. Kingdom wealth is about having godly success in all areas of your life. Never underestimate your ability and potential. You will never know just how much you have in you until you begin to develop yourself.

Self-development requires tools. One of the tools is people (relationships are very necessary for this to happen). We learn from each other. If there is something you want to learn, find someone that is doing it and glean from them. Remember, people are the greatest resource God has given to us. We cannot do this alone. By ourselves we are good, but together we are great! Don't settle for good when you can be great.

Step III—Self-Improvement

Endurance is one of the keys to success in the process of self-improvement. There is no success without self-sacrifice. Once you develop yourself, you must continuously improve. As I have discussed, we all were born with a gift, and your gift is what God has given you to take care of yourself. Your gift was given to you for a reason and a purpose. God knew that we needed to live and prosper, and your gift is what makes room for you and brings you before great men.

Your gift is linked to your increase and money. Kingdom wealth is also about accessing, developing, improving and using your gift for Kingdom enlargement. Self-improvement helps you master your gift, dominate your arena, multiply your resources, replenish yourself and be fruitful in every area.

Step IV—Application

Stagnation is an abortion chamber for your destiny and purpose. You will never succeed if you don't do something. The application of what we know, have learned and understand is necessary to walk in the abundance of God's blessings and favor. Productivity is of God. As discussed in Chapter One, when God created us, He blessed us with everything needed to be successful. All five blessings for success show us how to be productive. You cannot produce by doing nothing; and lack of application is considered doing nothing. When you tap into God's will and timing for your life, things will become effortless, and flow in such a way that will almost seem unreal. It is our responsibility to find the will of God for our lives and get in it.

When you apply the principle of God's word, you bring your outer self in harmony with your inner self. This causes you to flow in a realm of the Spirit that will produce manifestation—this manifestation is called Kingdom wealth. Accessing the Kingdom wealth of God will require action on your part. It starts with accepting Jesus as your Lord and Savior. This will lead to self-change, then self-development and, of course, self-improvement. The application will produce lasting results.

Many people want all of the wonderful blessings of God, but do not want to do what He requires of us to gain them. We are not only supposed to hear or know the word of God, but we must also live it. Applying the word of God in our lives is a sure way for us to experience the Kingdom wealth God has promised us. So many times we want God's blessings without His relationship. The relationship is necessary to have the wealth of His Kingdom. We cannot experience His Kingdom wealth without doing it His way. It must be God's will, God's word and God's way.

20 Keys for Accessing, Experiencing and Living In Abundance

I. **Abundant living requires:** a relationship with God through Jesus Christ

II. **Abundant living requires:** making the changes that God requires

III. **Abundant living requires:** a life of prayer, fasting and studying the word of God

IV. **Abundant living requires:** us to be obedient to the Holy Spirit

V. **Abundant living requires:** faith

VI. **Abundant living requires:** holiness

VII. **Abundant living requires:** us to obey the Word of God

VIII. **Abundant living requires:** the fruit of the Spirit to mature in our lives

IX. **Abundant living requires:** a healthy attitude

X. **Abundant living requires:** a selfless lifestyle, not a selfish one

XI. **Abundant living requires:** us to celebrate each other's successes

XII. **Abundant living requires:** motivation and confidence

XIII. **Abundant living requires:** us to continuously change and develop our character and work on our souls
XIV. **Abundant living requires:** us to be givers in every area of our lives: tithes, offerings, seed sowing, time, and talents, to the upbuilding of the Kingdom
XV. **Abundant living requires:** us to love; love is the giving of one's self away sacrificially without expecting anything in return
XVI. **Abundant living requires:** a life of gratefulness and not entitlement.
XVII. **Abundant living requires:** integrity
XVIII. **Abundant living requires:** patience
XIX. **Abundant living requires:** true worship; worshiping God with your lifestyle
XX. **Abundant living requires:** us to praise and bless the Lord at all times

Pray This Prayer

Father, I come to you in the name of Jesus Christ. I ask the Holy Spirit to impart into me more wisdom, knowledge and understanding of who I am in the Kingdom of God. Father, I ask you to forgive me for all the areas of my life that I have allowed to become unfruitful and lacking. I command the spirit of lack to be loosed from my life and I decree abundance to be bound to me now in the name of Jesus.

God, in the name of Jesus, I ask you to destroy every work of the flesh in my life. God, I come open and transparent before you now. God, I confess my issues and faults to you and I repent for every area in my life that I have sinned against you. I ask the Holy Spirit to search the innermost parts of my being, open me up in your presence, God, and wash me from every defiling thing that is in my soul. Holy Spirit, I ask you to mature the fruit of the Spirit in my life. God, I want to be free to live the life of abundance you have for me.

I release in my life the anointing of the tribe of Issachar so that I can rightly discern the timing and season. I speak to my spirit and command my mind, heart, will and desires to line up with my rightful season in God. Holy Spirit, stir up the gift of intercession in me and give me spiritual understanding on how to pray for my home, family, ministry, nation, country, states, citics, neighborhood and church, to see breakthrough in every area.

I ask you, God, to shift me into purpose and destiny that will bring me into my Kingdom wealth you have promised according to your Word and covenants. I war now in the Spirit for the release of finances and resources belonging to me. Attach my name to every resource that you have for me to accomplish my Kingdom assignment in the earth. I pray for all divine connections and relationships to be connected to me now.

Every blessing and promise that you have prepared for me from before the foundation of the world, I ask you to release it to come to me now without delay, in the name of Jesus. I call for the resources from the north, south, east and west—the four corners of the earth—to come now without hindrance or delay. I decree and declare that my barns will be filled and my purses will burst out with new wine of wealth. I release upon my life the anointing for increase, the enlargement of my territory and the broadening of my coast.

I decree and declare that provision will be made wherever I go. I thank you for favor with great men and that my gift is making room for me now. I thank you God that I have the Messiah's anointing of empowerment to work and do your will in the earth to enlarge your Kingdom. I thank you that I have the anointing of a warrior and I can go in and destroy my enemies and possess my land of promise.

I decree and declare success and progress in my life, ministry, family and finances from this day forward.

I thank you God that I have received my Kingdom wealth and I now live as a Kingdom citizen, accessing and experiencing every blessing you have for me, in Jesus Christ's name. Amen.

NOW, GO INTO PRAISE AND WORSHIP BEFORE THE LORD AND CONTINUE TO DECREE AND DECLARE THE WEALTH OF GOD IN YOUR LIFE!

MY SOLE PURPOSE FOR LIVING IS FOR THE GLORY OF GOD.

About the Author

Nicole K. Armstrong

Nicole K. Armstrong is an anointed prophet of God who preaches the uncompromising word of God with a powerful, prophetic utterance to the nations. She walks in an international anointing that shifts nations and regions for the Kingdom of God. She is a prophetic voice preaching a Kingdom message. Prophetess Armstrong is a much sought after conference speaker and has traveled extensively nationally and internationally with the message of Jesus Christ. Her upcoming projects include *Kingdom Worshippers* and *Kingdom Leadership.*

Prophetess Armstrong founded Nicole Armstrong Ministries (N.A.M.) in 2004 with two assignments: Sound the Alarm Prophetic Movement; and The Glory Encounter Gathering, a nationwide quarterly conference that will soon become an international phenomenon. Under the umbrella of N.A.M., she has founded Lady of Virtue (L.O.V.), a ministry geared towards educating, equipping and empowering women to walk in their God-given purpose around the world. She has also founded Kingdom Ministers Network, which is geared toward building character, teaching competency and uphold integrity; and Armstrong Publishing Company.

Prophetess Armstrong was born in Kingston, Jamaica. She relocated to the United States in 1985. She is a licensed and ordained minister under the leadership of Bishop Dianne R. Collins of Faith Walk Ministries, Inc. She has earned an Associate Degree and a Bachelors Degree in Biblical Education, with a leadership concentration from Beulah Heights University in Atlanta, GA. She earned her Master's Degree in Christian Counseling from the Pentecostal Theological Seminary in Cleveland, TN. She is currently a candidate for a Ph.D. in Christian Counseling and Theology. Prophetess Armstrong is the proud mother of one son, Nicholas Howard! Her life anthem is: "My sole purpose for living is for the Glory of God!"